SABBATH
ECONOMICS

SABBATH ECONOMICS

A Spiritual Guide to Linking Love with Money

Judith Wright Favor

ReadersMagnet, LLC

TABLE OF

CONTENTS

PRELUDE: DEAR READER vii

PART ONE
THE OCEAN OF LIGHT 1
  1. WAKING UP IN HAITI 3
  2. SEEING LIFE AS IT IS 9
  3. DRINKING WATER 13
  4. CARING TOUCH 15
  5. PASSING THE SALT 20
  6. TURNING THE TIDE 27
  7. LISTENING SPIRITUALITY 31
  8. RADIATING CHRIST 35

PART TWO
A LIVING STREAM **39**
  9. LOVE IS THE FIRST MOTION 41
  10. CONTEMPLATING MONEY 50
  11. WHERE ARE YOU? 54
  12. SLOWING: SABBATH REST 56
  13. OWING: DEBT AND DEFICIT 64
  14. WANTING STUFF .78
  15. SINKING DOWN TO THE SEED 88
  16. SPENDING: A SEARCHING INQUIRY 95
  17. SHEDDING: LETTING GO 99
  18. LISTENING INWARDLY 105

19. TENDING REGRETS, TUNING HEARTS . . . 113
20. PAUSING 120

PART THREE
FLUIDITY **125**
21. FRIENDS OF GOD, AND PROPHETS 127
22. WHERE IS THE BIBLE IN ALL THIS? 133
23. WHAT WOULD JESUS WRITE? 138
24. CHOOSING WHAT MATTERS MOST 145
25. KNOWING YOUR FLOW 149
26. GIVING YOUR BEST 161
27. WRITING YOUR STORY 168
28. BECOMING BOTH / AND 180
29. NEIGHBORING 183

PART FOUR
AQUIFERS **189**
30. TAKING STOCK 191
31. INVESTING IN JUSTICE 193
32. WHAT DO YOU REALLY WANT? 199
33. SOUL WORK .202
34. QUIETING 208
35. HOLDING IN THE LIGHT 213
36. MYSTERY OF LIGHT 220
37. WHAT RINGS TRUE? 224
38. HOW THEN SHALL WE LIVE? 233

POSTLUDE 237
RESOURCES FOR FURTHER EXPLORATION 245

PRELUDE:
DEAR READER

THERE ARE MANY WAYS TO approach a book like this one. We all tend to bring our own experiences and needs to whatever we choose to read.

If you are an interactive reader, you may gain a greater understanding of your own views and values, choices and decisions through themes, quotations and images in these pages.

If you are a reflective reader, you might pause periodically to reflect on where my experience matches yours, and differs from it.

If you are an inquisitive reader, you are likely to not only question my premises and conclusions, but also consider what you already know about love, money, spiritual guidance and scripture and try to predict where I am going with all this.

If you are a contemplative reader, you may want to linger over some favorite spiritual practices and experiment with a few new ones.

If you prefer personal narratives, you might skip the questions and go straight to the stories, easily identified by the subheading *Story*.

If you like to explore your hidden dimensions through dialogue with another, you may highlight *Paired Sharing* suggestions, or underline *Questions for Reflection* to discuss with a spiritual companion.

If you like to figure out where you stand on topics of love, money, soul-work and service by comparing your inner landscape to someone else's thoughts and feelings, you may find yourself focusing on the contrasts and similarities you discover in the experiences of others.

If you grow best by confiding in your personal journal, you will find plenty of provocative writing prompts.

Some readers will focus on ideas, intent on gaining the fullest understanding of my most important points.

Some readers will follow emotions, entering with empathy into the hearts of characters you meet in these pages.

Some will attend to personal relationships, intent upon the conflicts that tend to dissolve relationships and the practices that deepen them.

Some will find meaning in sensory experiences recounted here, visualizing settings, hearing voices and touching textures inherent in love and money interactions.

Readers engaged in ministries of listening, teaching, pastoring and spiritual companionship may be interested in the inner movements experienced by people who move from simply being *friends of God* to becoming prophets in the larger world.

Financially, whether you are *struggling to make ends meet* or are *just getting by,* whether you consider yourself *decently comfortable,* have *more than enough,* or have inherited millions, this book could be for you, if you want to do the most you can with what you have.

Spiritually, whether you belong to a well-organized religious tradition, a semi-organized bunch of meditators or are religiously unaffiliated, this book is for you if you hunger to discover deeper dimensions of your *heartmindbodysoul.* Readers who are not members of the Religious Society of Friends will learn a lot about the faith and practice of Quakers.

Erotically, whether you consider love to be a spectator sport, a partnership of passion, or a solo communion — and whether your amorous journey is a faint memory, a throbbing reality or a distant hope — this book is for you, if you want to touch the more sensory aspects of linking love and money.

Many of you will pick up the book periodically rather than reading it from beginning to end. Start with themes and stories that spark your interest. This is an interactive book, so I invite you to try out any spiritual practices that beckon. Respond to all, none or a select few of the multiple queries that salt most of the chapters. Write solo in your journal and / or ask someone to reflect with you conversationally in paired-sharing. Join a circle of trust if you feel led to do so, or form a new circle of your own.

Whatever your economic, political, spiritual or erotic situation, the stories that follow will offer fresh insights into the varied meaning of faith and practice. They may call you to invest greater attention and intention in loving self, God and neighbor as you increase your current quotient of empathy, compassion, self-awareness and service.

Whatever your mind-set, the process of questioning almost everything you hold dear about love and money may also prompt you to acknowledge your true wealth, and expand your imagination in creative ways to use it. Your unique talents, treasures, time and tenderness make a huge difference in our hurting world.

PART ONE

THE OCEAN OF LIGHT

WAKING UP IN HAITI

IN JANUARY 1990, I ACCOMPANIED a dozen privileged white American Christians to the island of LaGonave, off the coast of Port-au-Prince. We sat in a circle of Haitian street vendors, known as market women, or *ti machan*. They squatted easily on their haunches, while I tried to keep my balance on an upturned plastic bucket. When they joined voices in a hymn, I was moved to tears. Hard-working women began each weekly gathering by praising the Creator in harmonic Creole, faces shining with love for God, self and one another.

Each woman scratched out a living by selling daily necessities from a roadside blanket. Each purchased her initial stock of goods — soap powder, yams, salt, mangos, sewing needles — with a start-up loan from a Fonkoze community fund, the Haitian version of micro-credit, the successful model that Grameen Bank had founded a few years earlier in Bangladesh.

Sweating in the humid air, I was captivated to hear reports of their gains and losses, as translated by John, our guide with Beyond Borders. One mother reported good sales; she was overjoyed to end the week with enough money to pay her child's school fees. The others cheered and thanked God for her good fortune. Another woman had a sick father, so she had missed three days of selling to stay home and care for him. She was unable to contribute her weekly repayment to the community loan fund, so the others chipped in to cover her share.

My physical discomfort faded from awareness as I watched and listened to these women. I was uplifted by the fruit of their faith, so evident in the delight with which they supported each other in money and love. I learned much more than a just a fiscal technique that day. I was exposed, for the first time, to a lifestyle of mutual consent, engagement and solidarity between the poorest people in the Western hemisphere. It was inspiring to witness love in action among uneducated women, human beings who had each other's backs in the slow crawl up from misery to sustainability. Bonded in mutual effort, they shored each other up emotionally and spiritually as they gave to and received money from their shared modest fund. That day in Haiti, I felt palpable signals of embodied hope as the women closed their gathering by harmonizing with each other in yet another hymn of thanks and praise.

That night I half-slept on a mat of banana leaves, enclosed in a woven-stick shelter buzzing with mosquitoes. The next morning, my hostess squatted beside a charcoal fire, cooking a rice porridge that required continual stirring. When I offered to stir, she flipped a plastic pail for me to sit upon, and handed me the spoon. A bit later her daughter arrived from the river with a bucket balanced on her head. After breakfast, she poured a pint of water into a pink plastic basin and I gratefully bathed, recalling the Creole proverb about economic privilege: *A rock in the water cannot know the misery of a rock in the sun.*

Exposure to the realities and resilience of Haitian peasant men and market women changed everything for me. My prayer life shifted from occasional to urgent. Immersed in daily challenges faced by the poorest of the poor in Haiti, I saw the light of Christ in radiant faces and heard the Holy Spirit singing in many voices. A single two-week immersion was not enough. I followed the call to go back to Haiti annually in fourteen of the next eighteen years, introducing different groups of privileged white American Christians to our Caribbean neighbors.

Co-leader Dale and I balanced the group's busy days of

community service. Some tended children in Mother Teresa's orphanage, while others cared for dying women at *San Fils*. Each morning and evening we gathered at Visitacion House for a supper prepared by Ron Voss, a Jesuit ex-pat committed to freedom for the people of Haiti. We also began and ended each day in circles of prayer and sharing. We completed each immersion period with a 24-hour silent retreat in which we offered our participants a cared-for silence in which to reflect upon all they had experienced. This full-day pause was intentional, a bridge of stillness for *bodysoulheartmind* to metabolize the realities of Haitian poverty before returning to the realities of consumer excess in the United States.

But over-exertion then quickly caught up with me at home. Taking care of others while neglecting myself fueled a martyr reaction. I turned to wine and addictive eating, behaviors that left me feeling trapped in shame. Harmful choices turned out to be a pitiful substitute for real self - care. I had forgotten Jesus' Great Invitation: Love your neighbor and your God *as you love your self.* I discovered the hard way that — for me — periods of activism must begin and end with longer periods of cared-for stillness. I came to learn that it was the only way I could sustain the work of justice over the long haul.

When people like me — and maybe you — choose to nurture a contemplative posture in our financial lives, we become attuned to multiple methods of linking love with money. This book, this spiritual guide, offers a variety of ways to move from surviving to thriving in daily life, particularly when serving neighbors trapped in poverty. My choice to immerse myself in covenant circles certainly sprang from my love for God — and God's love for me.

And it did not take long for me to discover that contemplative spiritual practices are absolutely essential whenever we follow the call to drench our hearts and minds in the needs of a hurting world.

———————

Back home in California, I soon found that wordy ways of prayer no longer fed me. To stay true to an evolving vocation, I needed even more silence, more solitude and more stillness to absorb the presence of the Beloved. I'd be lying if I said cultivating mindfulness and heartfulness comes easy. These are demanding spiritual disciplines. I gave up on them several times, but now mindfulness comes effortlessly when I remember to take deep inhalations and even deeper exhalations. Making friends with a variety of practices from a wide range of spiritual traditions strengthened me to take on the tough personal challenges of fiscal indebtedness, household clutter and social inequality. Now I can count on daily contemplative practices to dependably empty out my emotional garbage and mental debris.

Annual pilgrimages to Haiti forced me to become more honest with myself. I could no longer ignore my unconscious ways of dealing with love and money. Personal relationships often got tangled. Confusion and denial darkened my relationship with money. I was ashamed of owning too much stuff, even as I sensed what I have come to call "Something More" beckoning me to shed stuff and give money. I wrestled with my own shadow by studying the Enneagram — a psychological/spiritual wisdom approach to self-awareness and growth — and it revealed long-hidden motives behind my behaviors. Each January, as I shared visceral experiences with Haitians, more personal flaws were exposed to the light. It is never easy to embrace all that we are — the good, the bad and the ugly –but it *is* possible. And it is good.

———

Repeated pilgrimages prompted me to leave my work as a parish pastor in San Francisco and embark upon a contemplative vocation. I meditated with seekers. I received moments of clarity in times of collective stillness, which eventually led me to find a new home among Quakers. A fresh vocation took shape when I was called to lead quiet days, contemplative writing and silent retreats sponsored by the Pacific Center for Spiritual Formation in the Bay Area. After I moved to Southern California, I was hired to offer soul care and spiritual formation ministry with seminary students at Claremont School of Theology and Stillpoint, a community of those known as Spiritual Directors, in Pasadena and New Mexico.

Eventually I found the courage to put my views, values and convictions on the page, embarking on a fresh ministry of writing for publication. Actively seeking divine guidance and deeply listening to God's "still, small voice" led me toward the "something more" of helping others to find freedom *from* debt and freedom *for* love -infused service in the world. It takes great intention and attention to live into something so large, and it also takes practice.

This spiritual guide is about "something more."
More than gaining, losing, saving or spending money.
More than finding or losing love.
More than managing budgets or debts or divorce.
More than negotiating the joys and woes of love
relationships.

This spiritual guide is dedicated to all those who
seek help to repair some of the love-money damage
sustained in early life.
These chapters are intended to shine light on the

"something more" within each reader right now, the
essence of which is right there in your essential nature.
There is a good reason you are here on Earth.
There is good reason you struggle with money-love
challenges.
And there is good reason you picked up this book.
These pages are meant to help restore you to the life
you are meant to live, by illuminating aspects of the
"something more" that may be eluding you.

I wrote this book from a personal leading rooted and grounded in a transformational love. These words emerged from a call to live with greater meaning and purpose by staying attuned to divine assistance. My own awakening happened in Haiti, and it took more than a decade of practice to find my way. The stories and questions and practices in these pages are soaked in life force. Perhaps they will shine a light on your path as well, that you may find ways to infuse compassion into your own money matters.

Money-love work can be hard, no question about that. It takes commitment and courage to delve into the hidden parts of our selves that lurk in the unconscious. Community support is vital when we undertake the inner work of self-reflection about love and money. So are circles of trust where you can share the inevitable doubts, difficulties and discoveries with others. May you, dear reader, seek here — and indeed find — clues to the "something more" that beckons you toward greater meaning, purpose and fullness of life.

SEEING LIFE
AS IT IS

You cannot say more than you see.
> – Henry David Thoreau

HAITI: DAY ONE

MY EYES BURNED AND LEAKED as our battered van lurched along crowded dirt roads, from the Port-au-Prince Airport to Visitation House. Thoreau's cool words came to mind, but did not ease eyes clogged with diesel fumes, dust and wrenching poverty.

My eyes protested in pain to see women with empty eyes, hair wrapped in head-rags, slumped in the doorways of hovels.

My eyes wept to see ragged men leaning against coconut palms at the edge of the road, staring listlessly into the dirt.

My eyes leaked at the sight of boys running beside the van, jumping up and waving sticks of gum for us to buy. In the eyes of these skinny boys, I saw desperate hope to receive a few *gourdes* or *kops*. (5 *gourdes* is the equivalent of one American dollar. 5 *kops* equal one cent.)

In sidelong glances from weary adults, I saw hopelessness. Haitian eyes — sometimes called windows to the soul — are smudged with suffering. In response, mine leaked without permission. I did not sob, but my eyes had empathy pains.

Systemic poverty is not right. It's not fair. Protest formed a knot in my throat. Later, I mentally complained to Thoreau. *You had it easy because you never came to Haiti. This is too much.* I now saw so much more than I could say!

Christ, have mercy on all of us. Help them survive. Help me bear the unseeable pain of a people who have endured generational poverty since 1697.

At Visitacion House, I took two aspirin, but the pressure-headache pounding behind my eyes did not let up. As I rested on the bed with a cool washcloth covering my over-heated eyes, I imagined Jesus addressing people like me, blind to the suffering of countless brothers and sisters. The Living Christ was now giving me eyes to see. Help me, I prayed. Keep my eyes open to life *As It Is* on this island patch of earth.

Before falling into a restless sleep, I imagined standing beside Jesus as he gazed out over Jerusalem, weeping in sorrow at what he sees. I realized I am not the first, nor will I be the last American Christian, to journey to Port-au-Prince in hopes of easing the steady suffering borne by Haitian children, youth, women and men. Help me remember we are all children of one loving God. Help us find ways to strengthen one other through presence and prayer.

The next morning, I asked a Haitian driver how to say, "I see you" in Creole.

"*A pi ta,*" he answered with a big smile.

"*A pi ta,*" I replied and smiled in return. *Mesi.* I see you, too.

In the van the following day, headed for my workstation at *San Fils,* Mother Teresa's Hospice for the Destitute Dying, I did keep my eyes open. This time, I noticed the bright eyes of a woman carrying a rooster on her head, and the weary eyes of a man carrying a pallet of bricks on his back.

I also noticed windows. Broken glass littered the ground in the business district. The more I looked for windows, the fewer

I saw. Metal grillwork covered most shop entries. Occasionally, I spotted louvered-glass slats in hotels and cafes. Open-work concrete blocks provided the most common window-like openings, as I found at *San Fils*, but there are hardly any glass windows in Port-au-Prince.

As the van labored up a long hill toward the hospice, my focus turned to prayer.

Help me, Christ.

Help me to be a channel for your healing power.

Help me ease suffering by massaging hands, feet and heads of women suffering from AIDS, cancer and God knows what other ills.

Help me communicate in my rudimentary Creole with patients who do not understand my language.

Help me release their pain whenever possible.

Help me bring a measure of comfort to women whose families can no longer tend to their medical needs.

As poet e.e. cummings predicted, *the eyes of my eyes were opened* in the course of that day, and continued through the fourteen years of listening, learning, praying and playing with a wide range of Haitian people.

On Day One, while still blinded by categorical thinking, I viewed all Haitians as "the poor." My vision was clouded by general categories. The homeless. The jobless. The oppressed. At first, I thought the eyes of the entire culture were clouded. Eventually, I came to see that the mote was in my own eye.

Haitians are humans, not categories. Haitians are individuals, unique people created in the image and likeness of God. They have suffered — and continue to suffer — under short-sighted, greed-driven leaders. Sinful human choices keep an entire society impoverished. Dictators abused power. Government officials practiced corruption. Military and economic impositions led to widespread oppression.

And yes, many Haitians do have poor eyesight. Dim vision is partly caused by malnutrition and inadequate medical care, but most is due to simple eye problems that could easily be corrected. Only rich Haitians wear glasses. Only the very wealthy wear contact lenses. Only the wealthiest of the wealthy can afford corrective eye surgery. The rest go blind from cataracts or macular degeneration.

Only men in power — uniformed, gun-toting members of the paramilitary *Tan-Tan Macoutes* — wear wraparound mirrored sunglasses. Ordinary Haitians cannot afford even cheap sunglasses, so their eyes have no protection from relentless rays of Caribbean sun.

What they don't see, they can't say. Thoreau got that right.

DRINKING WATER

I was thirsty, and you gave me something to drink.
— Matthew 25:35

CLIMBED THE METAL STAIRS AND entered the women's ward of *San Fils*, where the air smelled strongly of bleach. The unpainted concrete floor gleamed with damp spots from a recent mopping, for the Sisters disinfected everything every morning.

A patient near the door greeted me in a whisper.

Bonjou, Madame. Kijan oe ye?

She lay on a thin mattress atop a narrow metal cot. Her frail body was covered with a single blue sheet. She had no pillow. She seemed too weak to lift her head, but acknowledged my presence with her dark eyes, her beautiful, sorrowful eyes.

Bonjou. Mwen pas pale Creole, I stammered. Good morning to you, too. I wish I spoke more of your lovely, lyrical language, but I only know a few phrases.

A woman on the far side of the room raised a thin hand and gestured me near. I moved in her direction, carefully making my way between metal cots placed so closely together that I barely had room to slide sideways between them. This patient was younger than most, all skin and bones. She was curled in a fetal position, covered with one blue sheet. Our eyes met, hers smudged with pain. Her face was badly scarred; it looked as if she had been badly burned. She lifted a bony finger and pointed toward the pink plastic drinking tumbler perched precariously on the railing of her bed. The number 27, painted in red nail polish on the cup, matched the 27 painted on the head of her bed. So this was how the Sisters kept track of their patients.

"Are you thirsty?" I asked in English.

Patient #27 nodded 'yes' with a slight movement of her head.

I picked up her cup and walked to a forty-gallon trashcan of fresh water in a front corner of the ward. I spotted a small pitcher on an open shelf, bathed in sunshine flooding through the open door. Flies buzzed about, and I waved them away. I removed the lid from the water container, dipped in the pitcher, tipped water into the pink cup, and carefully replaced the lid.

I retraced my way through the ward, stepping carefully between the tightly-spaced cots lest I spill a drop. Clean water is a precious commodity in this thirsty land. The patient was too weak to sit up, but did unfold from her tight fetal position. I crouched beside her and cradled her head with one arm. Our bodies touched, and I felt her hot, feverish skin against mine. I tipped fresh water toward her mouth.

She drank and drank and drank, draining the twelve-ounce tumbler. *I was thirsty and you gave me something to drink.* I silently gave thanks to God for this clean water, for hospice care provided by the faithful Missionary Sisters of Charity, and for the gift of being right here, right now, holding this scarred and suffering soul.

She whispered *Mesi,* then closed her eyes, and curled back into fetal pose. I rose, rebalanced her pink tumbler on the railing at the head of her bed, and gazed down. Her face was furrowed with pain. *God have mercy. Christ have mercy. God have mercy.*

CARING TOUCH

Why do you take people in off the streets? people frequently asked Mother Teresa. Every time, she said the same simple words: To love them into heaven

EACH MORNING AT 9 AM, Sister Immacula and Sister Kamal unlocked the gates of *San Fils* and gestured us to step inside. Three American volunteers joined two Missionary Sisters of Charity, who came from India, to tend the needs of seventy destitute dying women. Their hospice is known as *San Fils*. The Creole name means *without family*.

Among the Haitian people, family is sacrosanct. Ancient voodoo practices have traditionally elevated family loyalty above all other values. Among Haitian Catholics, entire extended families deprive themselves of Eucharist whenever a daughter suffers an unwed pregnancy, for family loyalty requires everyone to publicly share her shame.

In times of sickness, families make huge sacrifices to care for one another, but the ravages of AIDS had exhausted meager resources. Many families had no choice but to bring their wretchedly thin, starving women to *San Fils* under cover of darkness. Maria, Dolores, Celia, and Marguerite are among those who were left at the gate during the night. It is too shameful to be seen abandoning a mother, sister, or daughter in daylight. Each morning, Sister Immacula finds yet another critically ill, emaciated woman lying in the road outside the gate. Being abandoned by one's family is the most degrading form of poverty. Being left to die at *San Fils* is excruciatingly humiliating for the patients, but everyone is treated with tender care. Missionary Sisters of Charity follow the example of their founder, Mother Teresa. *Faith in action is love and love in action is service.*

NOTES FROM MY JOURNAL
January 14, 1991

I feel competent when feeding gruel to patients, but incompetent when someone waves me away. I get hot when doing healing touch, not just my hands, but hot all over.

I felt alert when Marguerite, who'd been distant and distrustful, tried to sit up. She made eye contact and beckoned me to come. I saw the presence of Christ in her eyes as I massaged her face and head. Tears came for both of us in the face of her silent pain.

I felt at risk when Marie coughed frothy sputum onto my sleeve, and grateful for a good immune system and rubber gloves. I felt centered and clear as I held her head in my lap, held the basin for her vomit, wiped her mouth and crooned in sync with her moans. I was startled when she grasped my hand and placed it in the cavernous hollow of her belly. She demonstrated what she needed by moving my hand in small circles on her abdomen. When I did it just right, she closed her eyes and sighed.

I was touched to see three weak women offering tender care to a premature baby born here during the night. The mother must have died in childbirth, but two patients took turns feeding milk from a medicine dropper to the newborn, while another woman made a swaddling wrap from pillow stuffing and a frayed towel. The baby never cried.

An assertive young woman named Junia gestured me to come to her cot, flipped onto her stomach and pulled the sheet down to mid-thigh. I gasped at the scars on her buttocks, deeply ridged scars, pale against her black skin. She urged me to massage, but I hesitated. She grasped my hand and pressed it into scar tissue. Reluctant to hurt her, I pressed gingerly, trying to not imagine the kind of torture she must have endured. Harder, she gestured. I took a deep breath and went deeper. Belly-down on the cot, she sighed and wriggled with evident pleasure. Her erotic noises and movements made me feel uneasy. Patients in nearby cots were watching. I got self-conscious and stopped, but she objected. Keep massaging, she insisted, so I did. After a bit, it dawned on me that this damaged woman surely deserved whatever pleasurable sensations God provided for her, after the unspeakable abuse she had endured.

Thanks to you, Gracious God, for the privilege of being here to touch and be touched by these women who are beloved in your sight.

Looking back on that day, I confirmed that "grace-full" touch is always consensual, welcomed and enjoyed by all who share it. You and I know instinctively, when we are touched, whether we are being mishandled and manipulated, or caressed and cherished. A physical embrace may express dominance or equality. Being touched can diminish our self-respect, or it can also be sacramental, an outward and visible sign of an inward and invisible grace.

CARE QUESTIONS FOR REFLECTION AND DISCUSSION

Caring means taking delight in others, and in your self. How might you educate yourself in myriad ways of caring? I suggest starting by opening your journal and giving yourself quiet time to recall the forms of care you have experienced so far in life. God only knows what you might discover...

Reflective writing is a good way to become an expert in hands-on intelligence. When you listen to memories, recall your *bodymindheartsoul,* and record its wisdom, you will know exactly what to do when compassion calls on you to wrap your arms around a grieving neighbor, embrace a friend in pure joy, or even something like massage a stranger's scarred buttocks.

- Begin with your earliest memories and scroll forward to this point.
- How did your parents express their care for you? Cuddling, singing, playing? Conversing, giving gifts, helping with homework? Reading stories? Saying prayers? Baking cakes? Going swimming, camping, fishing?
- In what ways did you feel uncared for? How were you neglected or ignored? A latchkey kid? Told you were a nuisance? Yelled at? Physically abused?
- Who else cared for you as a child, beyond your family? In what ways?
- What forms of care did you give and receive in adolescence? Young adulthood? Tending, touching, teaching? Listening, mentoring, giving advice, giving money?
- How do you express care now? In what forms of care are you most skilled?
- Whose bodies do you care for now? How?
- Whose hearts, minds and souls? In what ways?
- What land do you care for? How?
- Which communities? Organizations? How?
- Who falls outside your circle of care?

- At what distance do you feel most comfortable with strangers? Colleagues? Friends? Family members? Lovers?
- Return in memory to a time before you were ten years old, and re-create for yourself the tactile and sensual environment of your home.
- What did your mother's body feel like? Your father's?
- Who touched whom? In what ways?
- Was there physical punishment? Violence? Sexual abuse?
- Record the smells you recall. Baby powder? Sheets fresh off the line? Tobacco? Whiskey? Baking bread? Soap? Perfume?
- What were the aromas of love? What did your mother smell like? Your father?
- What sounds pleased you? Irritated you?
- What colors did you find beautiful? Neutral? Annoying?
- What textures soothed or delighted your skin? Chafed it?

PASSING THE SALT

But if salt loses its zing, how will it be made salty?
Matthew 5:13b

CONTEMPLATIVE SERVICE IN A HURTING WORLD

WEALTH IS THE MOST CHALLENGING subject in the Gospels; we hardly know how to define it. Poverty and wealth are insidious themes throughout the Bible. Scripture is filled with paradox.

> *Too much and too little.*
> *Ease and unease.*
> *Isolation and community.*
> *Privilege and misery.*
> *Brokenness and wholeness.*

One message that shines through Jesus' teachings on love and money is how he used parables to provoke, challenge, and invite folks to rethink their attitudes. We may be born into poverty, but we can choose to live with generosity rather than misery. We may be born into privilege, but we can choose to use our surplus in serving others.

Core meanings embedded in Jesus' parables shine through these excerpts from a plenary speech given at the World Conference of Friends in Kenya in 2012:

I am Padip Kuman Lamichhane, 35 years old.

I live in the countryside of Kathmandu, Nepal, with my wife, five-year-old son, father, mother, and grandmother. I try to make a difference from where I am, happy to be able to feed my old parents and play with my son. I will do whatever I can 'til the end of my life to bring peace and joy to impoverished places.

Preparing to speak here to so many Friends is a tough job. It made my head heavy. I don't understand about theology, but this my small mind does understand: that God loves everybody and wants us to give saltiness and shine to the world.

I do not understand about trinity, but I know God is with me.

I do not understand about heaven and hell, but I know God loves me.

I do not understand what is sin, but I know God is full of mercy.

I do not understand clearly about salt, but I know I have to be salty.

I do not understand clearly about light, but I know I should shine.

I do not understand about different types of Friends, but I know they are all my Friends.

Hakuna matata means 'no worries.' Let us pray together.

I am touched by Padip Kuman Lamichhane's simplicity and his sincerity. I am inspired by his capacity to give *attention* to what matters most, and his capacity to form — and put into practice — his *intention* to make life better for those he loves.

I recently came upon one of my old journals, with these words scribbled on a green post-it note: *The act of giving is a polished gesture of generosity, inevitably wrapped in a wish to offer someone something they do not have.* I have no idea whose words I inscribed: maybe it was mine.

But I am pretty sure that if I were to tell Padip Kuman Lamichhane that I think those words describe him, this Friend from Nepal would surely shake his head and disagree.

Why? Because Padip shows no personal ego in the contemplative service he offers so freely. Generosity to his old parents and grandmother shines with Christ's Light. His saltiness comes from simply being fully attentive to what his son needs in the present moment.

He is more than half my age, yet it has taken me many long years to reach Padip's level of maturity. When I volunteered to tend dying women in that Haitian hospice, I did not shine with unselfish light. I was very self-conscious as I moved from bed to bed in the overcrowded Home for the Destitute Dying. I could speak only the most rudimentary Creole, so it was a challenge to figure out who wanted healing touch, who wanted silent companionship, who wanted a song and who wanted to be left alone. I may have outwardly appeared selfless and devout, but I secretly wanted to be praised for coming thousands of miles to help.

These unconscious motivations did not rise to awareness until I got home and had time to honestly appraise what was going on behind my pious face. When caregivers intentionally cultivate saltiness by praying with the Beloved five times a day, on their knees, as do the Missionary Sisters of Charity, secret desires come readily to awareness. Once any hidden motives are revealed by the light, they can be cleansed. Then caregiving truly shines with a truer generosity, as the nuns' shone. But for a half-baked Christian like I was in the Nineties, I had to spend long periods of "labor in the Light" before I could see my unconscious motivations.

Eventually, through the grace of God, I learned to notice, name and release those self-serving, ego-centered motives. Over time, I learned to establish habits of attention and intention that now reliably undergird me in contemplative service.

Pradip Kuman Lamichhane did it.

So did the Missionary Sisters of Charity.

So can you.

God works for good together with those whose habits of attention and intention equip them to offer selfless service in full accord with the teachings and actions of Jesus.

PAIRED SHARING

Find someone who is on the path of contemplative service in our hurting world, or someone who wants to be. Arrange a time when you can meet in a quiet place, free of kids and phones, to explore what saltiness means to each of you.

- Start with salt passages in Mark 9:50a, Luke 14:34-35a, and Matthew 5:13b
- When you think of a "salt of the earth" person, who comes to mind?
- Take six minutes to fully describe this salty person to your friend.
- Take two minutes to pause and reflect on what you heard yourself say.
- Take six minutes to listen as your friend describes the saltiest person s/he knows.
- Take two minutes in stillness to notice what was said, and not said.
- Take as much time as you like to add more details

about the "salt of the earth" people you know, and to talk back and forth about the salty aspects of your lives.

SHARING SALT: A STORY from KRIS in HAITI

You are the salt of the earth.

Matthew 5:13a

Soon after we returned home from one trip of perspective to Haiti, the island nation underwent a period of violent political instability. Armed gangs were attempting to overthrow President Aristide, and the U.S. State Department advised American citizens to get out. Kris, a volunteer with Beyond Borders, wanted to stay. She liked teaching at the Matenwa Learning Center on the tiny island of LaGonave, but did not want to put her neighbors at risk.

"How do you all feel about having an American living nearby during these uncertain times," she asked, during a staff meeting at the school. "What do you think I should do?"

Everyone went silent. Haitians frequently pause to think about things before they speak. One teacher said everyone would understand if she wanted to go home. Another said it would make them really happy if she felt comfortable staying. Another added that, although she could not predict how things might unfold, the local teachers would continue to teach the kids, and to support one another. "And we will support you, too, Kris," added the principal, "if you stay."

"I was thrilled," said Kris, "at how easy it was to reach my decision, knowing I had everyone's support. Then I began to receive frequent house visits from women in the neighborhood. In

Haiti, it is typical to drop by each other's homes now and then, but these visitors seemed more purposeful. Eventually I realized they were stepping up the frequency of their visits to show solidarity. People came by just to make sure I wasn't too sad, or too worried about the troubles.

"On February 27th, a larger-than-usual group of neighbors arrived on my porch. We shared news of our families as usual," said Kris, "but their mood was more somber. The island women told me they had lived through previous times of violence. They reassured me that the shooting probably would not reach our rural village, but warned that everyone was likely to go hungry if the supply boats could not sail from Port-au-Prince.

"When one woman said she was going to the market to buy rock salt, I said if we needed to start rationing food, salt wouldn't be the first thing I'd stock up on. They glanced at one another, wagged their chins and grinned. One neighbor said, "She doesn't get it."

What's to get? I was confused.

"Well, Kris," she told me, "rock salt is very important when there's no food. If you have nothing to eat, your body systems shut down, and that's when you're likely to get sick. But when you put rock salt under your tongue, it dissolves slowly and keeps the body going.

"That was news to me. We'd never gone hungry in Columbus, Ohio where I grew up, but my Haitian neighbors knew how to ease the risk of starvation, and they wanted me to do the same. I realized that these women were honoring me by teaching me how to live through famine, and by showing me how native Haitians support one another in difficult times."

"I did buy a little can of rock salt at market that day," said Kris, "but the next morning we awoke to news that the president and his family had been airlifted out of the country. For three days, no food supplies reached the island of LaGonave, but shipping resumed once the United Nations troops arrived to protect us. A can of rock salt remains on my shelf, reminding me of those courageous neighbors who guided me through difficult times. Solutions aren't easy, but we try to find them together. Neighboring may mean just listening, or discovering unexpected uses for rock salt. Solidarity means living in close proximity, walking in one anothers' shoes and gaining new vision as we meet new challenges together."

Kris continues to volunteer with Beyond Borders, working for justice and peace by fostering transformative learning within and across cultural and economic borders. One of countless people following God's call to contemplative service in our hurting world. Kris does not work alone. She is secure in knowing that her neighbors have her back.

TURNING THE TIDE

Koute = Listen
Pale = Speak
Li = Read
Eskrit = Write

WOMEN ARE THE BACKBONE OF the Haitian economy, but most do not qualify for loans at the banks, most of which are owned by Haiti's two richest families, because they lack collateral and therefore have no credit. Most street vendors, known as *ti machan,* never learned to read, write, add and subtract. Everywhere in Haiti, predatory "street bankers" make short-term loans to desperate vendors, and charge them 300% interest.

Fonkoze means *shoulder to shoulder* in Creole. Affordable, reliable cooperative credit for the working poor was a brand-new dream when Ann arrived in Haiti. The dreamer, Father Joseph, was looking for someone to guide the development of Fonkoze, someone skilled in management consulting, with leadership experience and a heart for the poor.

ANN'S STORY

Ann Hastings had recently retired as a management consultant in New York City. She had an expensive wardrobe, and dressed for success to help senior executives in government posts and non-governmental organizations become more effective. The work paid well, but the rat race wore her out. *I listened to them babble, and felt frustrated because I had no sense of mission,* she told me. In January 1996, she went to Port-au-Prince with CV in hand, to apply for a position as president of Haiti's biggest bank.

A lifelong Catholic, Ann met Father Joseph at Mass. He challenged her with piercing questions. *Who will you stand beside here? Will you stand with the wealthy power brokers, or with the organized poor? Most people are able to work and they want to work, but they need to know how to read and write and manage money. Where do you stand?*

Father Joseph was so clear and compelling that Ann could not resist saying she would consider his offer. *He gave me three minutes to eat lunch, put a typing table and paper in front of me, and began talking. Within twenty minutes I realized that this man had a great vision, but without a way in the world to make it happen. Father Joseph also said he had no resources to pay for my room and board, then patted my arm and said, 'I think you'll find a way.'*

Ann approached the Ministry of Money in Washington, DC, and the women there assured her that they knew people who would want to participate. *Just tell your story,* they advised, so Ann did. She raised $12,000 right away, and accepted the position as Director.

In the beginning, Fonkoze had just one office, located in a shabby part of Port-au-Prince. This is where I met Ann, when she was still learning to speak Creole. It was 1996, and she told of being daunted by the challenge of establishing micro-credit branches throughout rural Haiti. By the time we met again in 2002, Fonkoze had trained and equipped 130 workers and couriers to run fifteen rural branches, and only three were non-Haitian. Father Joseph's dream has been growing ever since.

"When I became Director, micro-credit was new to me," Ann said, "but I could feel the power of Father Joseph's vision, so I enlisted experts. 'Do you think Haiti needs a bank for the poor?' I asked. Yes, they said. And they taught us how to finance it through *socially responsible investing*. In 1996, we created Fonkoze USA, to channel private loans for the working poor in Haiti. We described what they needed, and people with surplus funds gladly loaned the money. In exchange, Fonkoze Haiti kept our American lenders informed about how the money was being used. (I, Judith, signed on early as a *relational investor* and continue to keep thousands of dollars pumping through the Fonkoze micro-credit economy.)

For five years Ann lived in a slum with a friend of Father Joseph, on a $6,000 per year grant from the San Carlos Foundation in California. She had no pension and no retirement plan.

In autumn 2000, a beloved colleague was kidnapped and Ann got a note demanding that she shut down Fonkoze if she wanted to save his life. The suspected kidnapper knew where Ann lived, so she took shelter at *San Fils* with the Missionary Sisters of Charity. They prayed with her for God's protection and guidance. Fonkoze had become a vital part of the economy. They had to keep the offices open.

The courier's tortured body was found sixteen days later.

Friend Ron Voss helped Ann locate a second-story apartment in a locked building. She relocated the Port-au-Prince branch of Fonkoze to another locked building just a five-minute walk from her apartment. Security guards accompanied her on the walk between work and home until that season of violence subsided.

FONKOZE'S STORY

Most Fonkoze clients are female, *ti machan* who have no education, for Haiti has no public school system. Most families are too poor to pay school fees, and most girls are not free to attend school because their labor is required at home to haul water, burn sticks into charcoal, look after children and tend pots on cooking fires.

Each new Fonkoze client received four months of literacy training, based on a model developed by Paolo Friere that combined literacy with the struggle for justice. Ann told me her clients loved a literacy game called *Jwet Korelelit La,* large cards printed with big letters, words & numbers in bold colors. Father Joseph gave her the first game in a brown paper bag. She published revised editions in white cardboard boxes, each filled with practical problems to solve, problems that required *Madame* to learn to do quick calculations in her head. Fonkoze clients formed teams to focus on the concepts, learn the skills and practice the reflection process. Very competitive, they named their teams after winning soccer teams — Argentina, Brazil, Chile, etc.

After successfully repaying their first loan and achieving basic literacy, Fonkoze clients then qualify for business training. They are then mentored in developing individual business plans based upon costs and profits, which usually qualifies them for larger loans.

The last time I spoke with Ann, in 2004, Fonkoze's next goal was to provide health insurance coverage to *ti machan,* where a small weekly fee would ensure them access to a local clinic.

LISTENING SPIRITUALITY

*To **listen** another's soul into a condition of disclosure and discovery may be almost the greatest service any human being ever performs for another... For in penetrating to what is involved in listening, do we not disclose the thinness of the filament that separates people listening openly to one another, and that of God intently listening to each soul?*

Douglas Steere

I T IS A TRANSFORMATIVE EXPERIENCE to be listened into what matters most, as Ann Hastings can attest. Father Joseph's probing questions and attentive listening animated Ann to move into unimagined realms. With divine assistance and human support, she became Director of Fonkoze, forming cohorts among the street vendors of Haiti, as well as successfully linking literacy with group micro-loans to thousands of *ti machan*

Attentive listening is also the heartbeat of contemplative prayer. When you and I choose to focus full attention on Love, our noisy thoughts learn to be quiet. Once the inner clamor quiets down, we hear more from the *still, small voice of God*. This voice often surprises us, because the One who *sends rain on the just and the unjust* has also been known to pour undeserved blessings upon folks like us.

Quakers *seek to know one another in that which is eternal*. When someone listens to me without judgment or coercion, I no longer need to hide my secrets, explain my ideas, or defend my actions. When someone hears me without imposing their blueprint of what I should think or feel or do… I become free to be myself. In the presence of a loving listener — who is also imperfect — I find that I no longer have to shore up my ego or hide my hurts. Warm, undemanding acceptance from another imperfect *soul-in-process* frees both of us to sink beneath the superficial stuff and dive into depths where Spirit moves, beyond our sight and control.

HOW DO WE DO IT?

> *I will show you hidden things,*
> *Hidden things you have not known.*
> Chant composed by John Philip Newell

One-to-one listening is simplicity itself. **Paired Sharing** opens us to the mysterious, healing force of God at work within and between us. When we genuinely hear and are heard, we are also likely to feel loved. Sometimes, we feel so profoundly loved that there are no words to express the truth of it. Heartful listening is the pivotal link in human efforts to connect love with money with relational growth with social change.

Listening spirituality has always been a core element in the Quaker *gestalt*. For nearly four centuries, Quakers have cultivated both inward and outward listening in pairs, and in groups. Friends developed the practice of **Worship Sharing** to help us remain mindful and expectant as we wait upon the potential emergence of the Spirit. It is different from what other religious traditions call *faith sharing*. Worship sharing involves focusing on a theme or topic, then responding to it. Among Friends, we speak more thoughtfully and succinctly in times of worship sharing than we do in ordinary conversation. Patricia Loring summarized it: *Worship sharing is an occasion for Friends to speak our minds and hearts on a particular subject, in the spacious context of listening for the Spirit.*

As in Twelve-Step groups, cross-talk is discouraged in Quaker worship-sharing, because social give-and-take dilutes prayerful attention and intention. Responding conversationally can easily devolve into competing, criticizing or patronizing. Among Friends, paired sharing and worship sharing provide safe settings in which everyone's views are received without comment, defense or attack. Attentive stillness and intentional listening foster an atmosphere of respect — the better to truly hear each other. This combination of attention and intention softens our defenses, opening us to trustworthy guidance from a Holy Source whose ways are beyond our ways.

QUESTIONS for REFLECTION and DISCUSSION

- What most fully nourishes my *heartsoulbodymind*?
- What spiritual struggles are taking up space in me?
- When I feel empty, how do I fill myself?
- One change I've made since the early days of my spiritual journey is…
- One habit of mine that might get in the way of spiritual listening is…
- What holds me together in hard times includes…
- Something I want to keep in the forefront of my attention is…

- One thing about me that prepares me to be an attentive listener is…
- One way I presently companion other people is…
- One awareness I want to nurture in coming days would be to…
- One next step would be to…

RADIATING CHRIST

Faith in action is love. Love in action is service.
Mother Teresa

My working-class Protestant parents taught me
to be useful, not decorative.
I was raised to be a capable girl, and to become a
self-sufficient woman.
I was taught to help others, but not expect help
for myself.
It was up to me to do the right thing, on my own,
without asking for assistance.

Now I am old. Finally, at eighty, I can question the efficacy of early lessons in self-sufficiency. Finally, I see the pride embedded in efforts to do everything for myself. I remind myself of my two-year -old grandson. Once, when I offered to help him with something, Andrew planted his little hands on his hips and declared, *Do it MYSELF!*

In old age, I can see how much shame is involved in acknowledging my own lacks and limitations. I wish I could say I have totally shed these shadows of stubborn self-reliance, but I can only say I am a work-in-progress. I do know one thing for sure: I am held in a web of love out of which I cannot fall. Now, when someone offers to help, I accept. Well, most of the time.

Once in a while I hear myself silently echoing little Andrew. I want to erase this stubborn streak, but it takes time. I want to learn — every time — to graciously say, *Why yes. Thank you.*

Under Covid-19 quarantine at the time of this writing, I shelter at home like everyone else, and practice more contemplative prayer. I also receive more offers of assistance than ever before. I suspect the radiant love of Christ *at work in me* is prompting younger friends to lend a hand. I can feel it gradually softening my pride and preparing me to accept even more radiant generosity.

Join me, if you wish, in energetically joining the Missionary Sisters of Charity. They recite this prayer each day, in many languages and in many places of shelter around the world.

RADIATING CHRIST

Dear Jesus
Help us to spread your fragrance everywhere we go.
Flood our souls with your spirit and life.
Penetrate and possess our whole being so utterly
that our lives may only be a radiance of yours.
Shine through us, and be so in us, that
every soul we come in contact with
may feel your presence in our soul.
Let them look up and see no longer us, only Jesus!
Stay with us, and then we shall
begin to shine as you shine;
so to shine as to be a light to others;
the light of Jesus, will be all from you,
none of it will be ours.
It will be you, shining on others through us.
Let us praise you in the way you love best
by shining on those around us.
Let us preach you without preaching,
not by words but by our example,

by the catching force,
the sympathetic influence of what we do.
Let us love in the evident fullness of
the love our hearts bear to you.
Amen.

QUESTIONS FOR REFLECTION AND DISCUSSION

- What is your daily practice?
- What keeps you centered and grounded?
- Is there a *common prayer* in your faith tradition that steadies and guides you?
- What might it look like to be intentional about practicing radiance?

PART TWO

A LIVING STREAM

LOVE IS THE FIRST MOTION

Our life is love, and peace, and tenderness; and bearing one with another, and forgiving one another, and not laying accusations one against another; but praying one for another, and helping one another up with a tender hand.

Isaac Penington

BECKY'S STORY

"I HEARD THAT THE GOVERNMENT CAN take away your kids if the heat gets turned off," whispered Becky.

"Tell me what's happening," said Marian, nudging Becky to the edge of the room where they could speak privately. Meeting for Worship was over, and Quakers were moving toward Fellowship Hall for coffee, snacks and conversation.

"I bought Christmas gifts for my kids," said Becky, "and paid the credit card bill in January, but couldn't afford to pay the gas bill. Money was still tight in February, so I put that bill in a drawer without opening the envelope. Yesterday I got a disconnection notice. The gas will be shut off Tuesday."

Snow covered Minneapolis. Another storm was predicted.

Before rushing to solve the problem, Marian listened with empathy. First she heard Becky's whole urgent story. Then she guided her in how to request emergency assistance from a community agency. Once the crisis had been averted, Marian brought together a Caring Concerns Committee to support Becky over the long haul. They offered practical help, arranged credit counseling and helped her develop a long-term plan to reduce debt.

Love was the first motion for Minneapolis Friends. The second motion was to form a covenant circle around Becky, so she didn't have to do it all alone. That's the best way to link love and money. It is one version of Sabbath Economics.

Ralph Waldo Emerson appreciated covenant circles such as this. He wrote, *to share often and much... to know that even one life has breathed easier because you have lived, this is to have succeeded.*

DEAN'S STORY

Dean needed to lose excess weight, but could never keep it off. He tells it this way: "I'd manage to lose twenty pounds, but it would come back on within a year. My co-worker Ian was overweight too. He challenged me to put money on the line to back up my intention. He called it a commitment bond. If I failed to meet my goal weight, I owed him money and he would give it to a charity of his choice. I took him up on it and put $500 at risk each week. The strategy worked. Before long, I lost 25 pounds. My weight remained remarkably constant for forty weeks.

"Eventually Ian got serious about his own weight loss. He posted a commitment bond to me, and it helped him lose 38 pounds in less than a year. Neither of us lost any money, and our combined life expectancy went up by almost five years."

Dean and Ian couldn't keep excess weight off without support. Colleagues in a Boston investment firm, they did not speak the love language of this book, but they did link mutual respect with friendly competition to support each other in reaching their health goals. I see commitment bonds as a secular version of Sabbath Economics. It's all about freedom.

Toni Morrison put it succinctly: *The function of freedom is to free someone else. If you are no longer wracked or in bondage to a person or a way of life, tell your story. Risk freeing others.*

CHARLOTTE'S STORY

Charlotte was born with a proverbial silver spoon, but the family wealth left her feeling socially isolated. She received a large legacy in midlife, which freed her *from* the need to earn a living. It also freed her *for* the chance to grow spiritually. Searching for ways to put her inherited wealth to work, she participated in Ministry of Money workshops. There she met Barbie and Mary, whose hearts were also expanding. The three women found a lot in common, and soon felt led to pool their surplus wealth by giving grants to support other women on spiritual journeys with their love and money.

The New England trio started small. They interviewed and funded women they already knew through personal and Quaker networks. Seven years later, these good stewards were ready to legally incorporate the fund and widen their reach. From then on, they enlarged the covenant circle by inviting each year's grantees to a retreat, wherein they heard everyone's stories and shared spiritual practices. After Mary's death, Barbie and Charlotte continued to host annual celebrative circles in order to honor the spiritual transformations funded by ongoing financial and prayerful surplus.

The elders didn't just bumble along as solo philanthropists. They formed a covenant circle to mutually discern their way forward, linking love and money to support spiritual and financial growth among younger women. They followed biblical guidance from First Peter 4:10, *Like good stewards of the manifold grace of God, serve one another with whatever gift each of you has received.* They practiced a very intentional form of Sabbath Economics.

SPIRITUAL, SECULAR AND RELIGIOUS

The root word for religion means *to tie* or *to link*. Sabbath Economics seeks to link timeless religious wisdom with enduring spiritual endeavors with secular *best practices* — in the quest to unite love, money and freedom.

Sabbath Economics can be viewed through any of three lenses, depending on what matters most to each reader. Some see it as a religious idea, some approach it as a secular practice and others claim it as a foundational spiritual process.

People traditionally view religion as a way to make sense of a confusing world, but religion gets mixed reviews these days. Spirituality holds more appeal for younger people, as in *I'm a spiritual person, but not religious.* Religion encourages belief in something beyond self, but also has historically oppressed people and dominated nature. Maybe that's why increasing numbers of folks define themselves as spiritual rather than religious. Spirituality seems roomier somehow, larger than the greed and violence embedded in some historic religions.

Where are you with all this? If you think religion has no influence over personal economics, however, check the contents of your wallet. Currency issued by the U.S. Treasury — every coin and every bill — bears two phrases. One is *United States of America.* Do you remember the other one?

Freedom in pursuit of a buck has been central to American

life since at least 1776. Our country was founded on the passion for life, liberty and the pursuit of happiness. This so-called *Jeffersonian trinity* summarizes our common inheritance and defines our common aspirations, but in recent decades a new truth has become self-evident: We, the people, have radically altered what our nation's founders meant by the *inalienable rights* named in The Declaration of Independence.

If one were to choose a single word to characterize the national identity, it would have to be MORE, said Andrew C. Bacevich. We have become consumed by consumer-driven mottos. *If it feels good, do it. Shop 'til you drop. Whoever dies with the most toys wins.* More citizens are claiming the right to consume more and acquire more while indulging in more personal choices, more comforts and more conveniences. Bacevich names this *the crisis of profligacy,* and proposes that the relentless pursuit of MORE has become the center of our national theology.

However, many Americans do choose to use our national freedoms to pursue worthier endeavors. You and I, and many dear ones, choose to create and contribute, invent and invest, rescue and restore. Many of us volunteer in worthy causes, others envision and institute more sustainable environmental practices. 21st Century citizens are once again redefining *the pursuit of happiness.* New possibilities with love and money are continually expanding, along with American waistlines and the national debt.

Collaboration frees us from chasing after more, hoping to eventually feel that we finally have enough. Fears of *not enough* are balanced by acts of mutual sharing. Reciprocity is as American as potlucks, quilting bees, play groups and carpools. Our people have always looked out for each other, sharing what we have to make a difference for those who have less. Collaboration is the circuitry through which monetary resources, energy and imagination flow: some see these as the forms of love that make the world go 'round.

In God We Trust is imprinted on every coin and bill we pass from hand to hand. Trust in *enough for all* is implicit in each action of cooperation and collaboration that we take. Mutual reciprocity is like the air we breathe. You and I inhale exactly what we need — no more — and exhale exactly what we need to release. And it is enough. Joining into covenant circles with like-minded folks frees us to make a difference with what we have. Circles of care put money in its rightful place, as one of many resources we have to offer one another. When we recognize our need for reciprocal relationships and shine the light of gratitude on circles of mutual giving and receiving, we illuminate vast reservoirs of wealth. And covenants keep our money moving, circulating through society purposefully, to do the most good for the most people, including for us. With reciprocity comes nourishment and joy. When we are there for each other, trust increases.

COVENANT CIRCLES

Contemplative faith and practice — Quaker-style — brings us to covenant circles. Friend Emily Provance's definition of covenant conveys its inherent sense of reciprocity: *We give ourselves to God and God, in turn, gives us to a group of people. And from there, we are expected to care for this group of people, and this group of people is expected to care for us. As a whole we are expected to be obedient to the will of God as written in a set of commandments. Among Quakers, this means faithfulness to the will of God as it is constantly revealed.*

Becky and Marian share covenant-circle prayer with members of Minneapolis Friends Meeting, and Northern Yearly Meeting. They belong to national covenant circles, including Friends General Conference, American Friends Service Committee, and

Friends National Committee on Legislation, as well as the global circles of Friends World Committee on Consultation.

Charlotte is in covenant with members of Dover Friends Meeting, and New England Yearly Meeting, plus larger Quaker circles listed above.

Mary and Barbie pray with members of Portland Friends Meeting, and New England Yearly Meeting, plus wide-spreading branches of the national and international Quaker tree. In addition, they form covenant circles with recipients of their grants, and join circles with Woman's Perspective division of Ministry of Money and many mission groups under the care of Church of the Savior in Washington, DC.

Covenant circles connect us across income-tax brackets, zip codes, ethnicities, national origins and languages. I don't know if Boston businessmen Dean and Ian are part of other religious or secular circles, but I hope they are. Circles of trust can make a world of difference as we work to sustain the lifelong challenges of linking money matters with hearts of love.

JUDITH'S COVENANT STORY

Prayer on behalf of others is mysterious, but fundamentally seems to be an opportunity to participate in divine love. In prayer, as we compassionately consider the condition of others, we come to know them and their needs better, learning to love and respond to them, perhaps becoming aware of some help we might offer… Our prayer for others may first be transforming for us, and a way to learn to join in the ceaseless self-giving of the Divine.

Marcelle Martin

I joined Claremont Monthly Meeting of The Religious Society of Friends on February 24, 2000, the day before my 60th birthday. This date means a lot to me because it took so long to find my people. I grew up Presbyterian and attended a Congregational college. I raised my kids in the Unitarian Fellowship. Drawn to monastic life, I considered becoming a Catholic so that I could live in contemplative prayer with the sisters of Redwoods Monastery. Meditation beckoned, so I went to Shasta Abbey, and learned Zen practices from Roshi Jiyu Kennet, the first female Buddhist leader in the United States.

It was at Shasta Abbey, during a *sesshin* in the *zendo,* that living Christ enfolded me in loving light one bright September afternoon. I heard just eight words: *These are not your saints. Come unto me.*

That got my attention. The wonder and awe felt too big to keep to myself, but I couldn't figure out how to explain it to the *roshi,* so I took counsel from Mother Mary and hid the amazing mystical experience in my heart. I held it as a "secret pearl of great price." At home, I did confide in my husband, but he mocked my divine encounter, and that hurt. I didn't have a minister, so I went to the university and asked a professor of religious studies for counsel. He didn't get it either.

I knew Christ was asking something of me, but I did not know what. Before long, the United Methodist Bishop sent a woman pastor to my town, the first female religious leader in Chico. I started attending worship services at Aldersgate church and cried every time Reverend Judith prayed, or blessed a baby in baptism, or said the benediction. She noticed my tears. *Let's talk,* she said. *Can you come to my office tomorrow morning?*

There she listened to my full account of mystical union with the living Christ. She recognized that Christ had called me into service and — astonishingly — asked if I would serve as her spiritual guide and pray for her ministry. After many months of counsel and my involvement in church affairs, she helped me to enroll in seminary. In Berkeley, at Pacific School of Religion, I prepared for service as a parish pastor in the United Church of Christ. And there is more to my faith journey, which you'll see in upcoming chapters.

So yes, it took me a long time to find the Religious Society of Friends, and I am eternally grateful to finally be a Quaker. The Friends see "that of God" in everyone, even me. Friends embrace each other in circles of profound silence, protecting space and solitude in which to hear *the still, small voice* of God, and to experience the peace of Christ that passes understanding.

I love belonging to a covenant tradition that goes back to the 1600s. My history with Friends spans only twenty years, but I do like to celebrate my *Quakerversaries*. Sometimes I share my gratitude during Joys and Concerns at the end of Meeting for Worship. Sometimes I simply gaze at photos snapped during my welcoming breakfast and smile back at the Friends who surrounded me twenty years ago, and still do.

What I did not understand in the year 2000 — what I did not yet have language to explain, even to myself — was how God had guided me through many circuitous routes to finally find The Religious Society of Friends. Nor did I yet understand that my longing for covenant circles was larger than personal. These pages are my best effort to describe my God-given leading to find words for the inexpressible. (I am so glad you're here to be part of the journey!)

CONTEMPLATING MONEY

Normally, when we talk about money, we are really talking about what to do about it. How to get cash, spend it, invest it, save it, pay taxes with it, or avoid paying taxes. Hate it or love it, rail against it or lust for it... money is a fact of life. Yet most of us understand money far less than we do most other 'facts of life.' And almost none of us choose to stand in its presence the way we do with a redwood or a Rembrandt. We may worship it, pay homage to it, or sacrifice our lives for it, but we don't contemplate it.

-Joe Dominguez

So, WHAT IS MONEY? WHAT are we contemplating when we contemplate money?

We could take bills from our wallet and coins from our pocket and place them on a small altar. We could sit down in front of the altar, straighten our spine, relax our shoulders, steady our breath and contemplate the "money" in front of us. But what we see is only the physical shape of our nation's currency. We can't eat it or wear it. In some parts of the world, we can't even buy anything with it. So, money must be more than paper and metal. But what, then, IS it?

To discover where we are with money, we need to go beyond "stuff" and explore the nonmaterial realm of money. This realm encompasses a *lot*, including:

- Paid employment and efforts to get a better paying job
- Where to buy healthy food and shop for quality clothes, electronics and cars
- How to manage credit cards and mortgage rates
- When to buy insurance — health, life, automotive, homeowner, disability, jewelry and long-term care
- How to figure out deductibles and riders and premiums
- Where to bank
- How to manage checking and savings accounts
- How to negotiate loans
- Charitable donations

Then there's investing:

- What's the difference between CDs and IRAs, Keogh plans and 501c.3s?
- Which is smarter — municipal bonds, Fannie Maes, Freddie Macs, junk bonds or futures?

Then there's tax planning:

- Retirement Planning
- Income Averaging
- Wills and Trusts
- Burial Insurance

How many of us learned this stuff in high school?

How many of these aspects of money are woven into the fabric of our family lives, or woven into the folk knowledge of our culture?

How much of it do we keep out of sight, out of mind?

Clearly, there is more to the realm of money than I have

mastered, so you won't find smart money management tips here. Why? Because I barely passed Economics 101. I earned A's and B's in most of my college subjects, but Economics was beyond comprehension. I expected to flunk, but managed to pass with a D-minus. Numerical dyslexia was a big part of the problem, but I didn't know that until diagnosed later in grad school, on my way to a Master's degree in Psychology. A statistics course was required, so I hired a tutor and still barely managed to squeak by. So, no, I am not an expert in money management. I get by with a little help from my friends, certified public accountants who keep me square with the IRS, and certified financial planners who handle my IRA and community investments.

Money is a complex, multi-layered topic. This spiritual guide offers a very personal approach to Sabbath Economics. The key to the kingdom is to closely examine each money thread in your own story, the invisible threads woven into the fabric of your fiscal past, present and future. Yes, your threads may be elusive, but they have meaning. Know that each thread is worthy of your attention.

If you want to go deeper into realms of money management, you'll find a wide range of authors listed in the *Resource* section. In order to keep your finances on the right track, you may need more professional guidance than these pages hold. I strongly recommend using the Financial Integrity Program Guide as a companion text while reading this book. (http://financialintegrity.org)

Delving into the mysteries of money with the support of a spiritual guide can also be a wise practice. Tender soul care offered by individuals and circles of support can be enormously helpful in aligning fiscal numbers with personal strengths, skills, and aspirations as you work to transform your relationship with money through love. And remember Gregg Levoy's warning: *The truth will set you free, but first it may scare the living daylights out of you!*

QUESTIONS FOR REFLECTION AND DISCUSSION

Sabbath Economics contemplates love and money through a four-fold focus on emotional, spiritual, mental, and financial relationships. Set aside a quiet evening to sit with these questions — and mine them for all they are worth.

- Did your family consider itself rich, poor or just average?
- Did your family's financial situation set you apart socially because it was less than, or more than, the families of your friends?
- How did you feel about that?
- Did you have an allowance?
- Did you earn it by doing chores?
- Did your parents say NO when you asked for something that cost "too much money"?
- How did that affect you?
- Were there arguments?
- Who handled the money in your family?
- Did you grow up in a family where money was discussed openly?
- Or was it considered impolite to talk about money matters?
- What messages about money did they give you?

WHERE ARE YOU?

I have called you by name, you are mine... because you
are precious in my sight, and honored, and I love you.
Isaiah 43:1 and 4, NRSV

LOVE ARRIVED LONG BEFORE MONEY was invented. In the beginning, the Creator loved Adam and Eve, back when the first couple were newly created and trying to find their way around the first garden. Both were bare, and barely acquainted, when The Most High tried to start the first divine-human conversation. Three chapters into Genesis (3:9), God asked a curious open-ended question. *Where are you?*

It sounds like a great way to invite Adam and Eve into relationship.

Remember how they responded?

But that was then.

You and I can choose a different way forward.

Dear reader, your mission, should you choose to accept it, is to imagine the God of Love asking you the same question posed to the first woman and man.

Where are you?

Envision yourself back in the garden. Maybe you're leaning against a tree, admiring the greenery. Perhaps you're hoping to eavesdrop on Adam and Eve. Maybe you, too, are searching for some kind of fig leaf when the voice of God suddenly breaks into the Edenic silence.

WHERE ARE YOU?

What tone do you hear? Is the voice kindly? Reassuring? Or commanding? Intimidating? Plenty of Bible stories describe people being terrified by the thunderous voice of the Lord King Judge. What do you hear?

In my mind's ear, God's voice sounds warm and friendly. Interested and curious. I hear the Creator reaching out to connect with human creatures, because I believe the Source of Love genuinely wants to know what is going on with us. You and I are complex creatures, designed in the image and likeness of God, the most complex Mystery of all. Curiosity goes a long way in building relationships of trust and love between humans and the Holy One.

Where are you? The question invites each of us to respond openly to the Beloved. An invitational spirit enfolds these pages and infuses this whole Sabbath Economics enterprise. Each story, each question and each spiritual practice in A Spiritual Guide to *Sabbath Economics: Linking Love with Money* is rooted in the lived reality of trusting relationships between holy and human, love and money.

If prayer, as my former spiritual director Jim Neafsy says, *consists in contemplative attention to what God is doing within us and around us,* we might best spend our entire time reading this book in a state of prayer.

SLOWING:
SABBATH REST

FROM SECULAR DOING to SABBATH BEING

The Sabbath is a bride, and its celebration is like a wedding.

Rabbi Abraham Joshua Heschel

TGIF! How MANY OF US have heard or said *Thank God it's Friday!* as we left the workplace? *TGIF!* is a widely-shared expression of relief in our culture. Thank God the work week is over! But does the pace of public and private life ever really slow down? How many of us are accustomed to enjoying life at a Sabbath's pace?

Most 21st-Century folks seem to work most of the time. *Time is money*, or so we say, a handy cliché to justify the restless pace we keep. Working hard to consume prepackaged leisure activities, many of us miss out on the restorative spirit of Sabbath. Body and soul get depleted, along with heart and mind. Forgetting the lightness of being, we remember the weight of obligations. It has become rather quaint to set aside a day of rest to rejoice in Holy Presence, but when we neglect to take our imaginations out to play, we often go bereft of creative ideas. Taking the time to savor memories from a friend's funeral seems as outdated as a porch swing. Deprived of Sabbath, we get no rest. Busy-ness rules our days. Time becomes a monorail that rushes us from one place to another. Those who honor the Sabbath are in the minority these days.

———·✦·———

The word Sabbath comes from the Hebrew verb *shabat*, which means *to rest or stop working*. God rested after six delightful days creating light and dark, land and sea, animals and humans (Genesis 2:2). The Creator of the cosmos established the primal pattern of good work followed by rest. It was very good for God to rest, and it is very good for us too. *This cosmic Sabbath was not for the purpose of resting in order to work more*, writes Ched Meyers, founder of the Sabbath Economics movement. *There is no Monday in the Creation narrative. The purpose of God's cosmic Sabbath is to enjoy the world forever, which is why it is blessed.*

Honoring the Sabbath gives people like us more than the righteous satisfaction of obeying an ancient commandment. The inner stillness of Sabbath opens the seeds of Essence within us. It frees loving-kindness to circulate through our bloodstreams. Sabbath rest cracks the shells of fear within us, freeing hidden seeds of trust to sprout and grow. Restful reflection eases ego's tight grip on us, healing old deficiencies and erasing old masks. Keeping the Sabbath holy invites our shy souls to emerge from the seed, share our spiritual gifts and become as fresh and vivid as a child. Playing and praying loosens our grip on social conventions. Contemplative reflection eases the hold that economic forces have on us. Hanging out with the Beloved unlocks treasuries of goodness and mercy within us, so that you and I can make a healing difference in this hurting world.

FROM EFFORTFUL STRIVING to SABBATH LOVING

C.G. Jung tells the story of a native African who was invited by American visitors to get into a car and take a drive with them. After half an hour the passenger asked the driver to stop. He stepped from the car and stretched out on the ground, resting his back against the soil. They asked if he was sick. No, he felt fine. It's just that the car had gone too fast and his soul was left behind. He had to wait for it to catch up.

The pace of secular society does race ahead of soul time. Sabbath practices and Sabbath economics help us keep soul and body together. They also help us notice when distance grows between the two.

In America, the dual purpose of life is to cultivate wealth and strengthen ego, right? Our culture and economy both seem to say so. Most people feel doubly driven. Secular social forces reinforce individual autonomy, subtly working to enhance and maintain personal ego, convincing us to work harder so that we can accumulate more security, more stuff and more success. This individualized way of life puts enormous pressure on you and me, even during so-called leisure time. Society compels us inwardly to build up our sense of self-worth, while economic pressures compel us outwardly to build up financial assets. When the dual pressure gets to be too much, we tend to collapse into some kind of oblivion through food, TV, sleep, sex, alcohol, drugs or whatever gets us numb for a while. How many of us do this, bounce between some form of driven achievement, on and off the job, and some form of mind-numbing private escape? Given this crazed socio-economic rhythm, is it any wonder many of us wind up feeling anxious and empty?

True Sabbath may not be easy to attain at first. Sabbath

practitioners need commitment to stay with it. Inner states of deficient emptiness and spacious emptiness are constantly changing places on the dance floor of our consciousness. Those who remain faithful to Sabbath practices affirm that regular rest and reflection do nourish the body faithfully, restore the soul, illuminate the mind, untangle the emotions, and free the ego from social pressure to release personal finances from patterns of over-spending and under-giving.

THE GREAT INVITATION: THROUGH EMPTINESS to ESSENCE

All I want to say to you is 'You are the Beloved,' and all I hope is that you can hear these words as spoken to you with all the tenderness and force that love can hold. My only desire is to make these words reverberate in every corner of your being — 'You are the Beloved.'
Henri Nouwen's letter to a Jewish friend

Spiritual emptiness has its difficult moments, but a Beloved enough-ness makes that effort worth the challenge. Jesus and Buddha both sought emptiness. Alone in wilderness, forest, garden, mountaintop or boat, Buddha and Jesus both practiced a form of self -emptying known as *kenosis*. Sabbath emptiness invites us to experience kenotic freedom directly by dwelling with Essence. In sacred emptiness, everything is enough and we, too, are enough. When you and I can stop working so hard and be still, surprising blessings flow from the Source of Life. When we allow universal Light to clear our minds of "brilliant ideas," mental clarity freshly illuminates our concerns. When we let Love empty us of emotionally-charged *he-said/she-saids*,

Transforming Power can ease the difficulties in love relationships. When we allow Sabbath rest to support us in detaching attention from external distractions, Holy Spirit can restore us to physical aliveness. When we give our willpower a rest from planning tomorrow's agenda, divine guidance may point us toward the next step on the path of right action.

What do I mean by Essence? Essence, the unchanging nature of Love, is the inner seed of God at the core of each human being. Jesus introduced four dimensions of essence in a teaching that biblical patriarchs termed The Great Commandment (Luke 10: 25-28). I prefer to think of it as The Great Invitation, because the ministry of Jesus was essentially invitational. During his ministry on Earth, the Teacher from Nazareth invited us into the fourfold wholeness of loving self and neighbor (near and far, known and unknown) as we love God: with all our heart, soul, mind and will. Eugene Peterson's *The Message*, a contemporary version of The Holy Bible, translates it this way: *Love the Lord your God with all your passion and prayer and muscle and intelligence — and love your neighbor as well as you love yourself.*

Scripture writers testify to the Something More that infuses people with joy, compassion and patience. The Prophets tell of ordinary women and men who shine with honesty, generosity and peace. The Psalmist praises God for gifts of intellect, imagination and vision, expressing wonder for pleasures of sight, hearing, taste and touch. Passion, prayer, muscle and intelligence are meant to work together for the greater good. Inward listening invites the Source of Love to fill us from the inside, which then releases our will to receive intuitive guidance and take right action.

A CONTEMPLATIVE SABBATH PRACTICE: FREE TO ACCOMPLISH NOTHING

How beautiful it is to do nothing and then rest afterward.

Spanish proverb

If my Puritan ancestors had heard this proverb they would have scoffed and dismissed it. My forefathers and foremothers were Scot/English farmers, truckers, cooks and gardeners who extolled the virtues of hard work and self-denial. Along with fair skin, I inherited the family motto *Be useful, not just decorative.* Children in my blue-collar, working-class family were instructed to *Keep busy or at least look busy.* Doing nothing is still quite a challenge for me. How about you?

To honor my steady, sturdy ancestors, I can choose to accomplish nothing today in a way they would be capable of understanding. Your mission, should you choose to accept it, is to accomplish nothing. Just for today, I invite you to join me in practicing The Great Invitation of Jesus. Can you enjoy a do-nothing day — or at least a do-nothing evening — in which you simply let yourself be fully loved by the Beloved?

If *nothing-doing* seems totally impossible, you might play with some simple variations.

Let your eye muscles relax as you watch the grass grow.
  Let your ear canals rest as you listen to melodic music.
    Let your hands stretch as you play with a yo-yo.
      Let your brain strain dissolve as you gaze at the sky.

Or — find a place where you can stand comfortably on the earth, a spot where you won't be disturbed for a while.

Take off your shoes and go barefoot if you like.
Plant your feet a comfortable width apart.
Let your body find its center of gravity and simply enjoy being
rooted and grounded in the soil of this good earth.
Notice what comes up for you.
Take as much time as you like or need.
Invite imagination to be your guide
Then curl up and take a nap.

Henry David Thoreau became quite accomplished at accomplishing nothing. When peers accused him of idleness, he described its deep virtues in *Walden*. Playfully reversing the ancient wisdom recorded in The Book of Genesis, Thoreau declared: *It was morning, and lo, now it is evening and nothing memorable is accomplished.* Thoreau's enduring words testify to the myriad, mysterious ways in which *nothing* is transformed into *something* during open, unstructured times of Sabbath. Letting go of busy agendas is very freeing. Accomplishing nothing lets us discover our true place — personally, relationally, economically, environmentally and spiritually — as we honor the Sabbath and keep it holy.

SABBATH RENEWAL

Love the Lord your God with all your heart, with all your soul, with all your strength, and with all your mind, and your neighbor as yourself.
Luke 10:27, JB

Personal peace and global justice are rooted in economic stability. Given the relative affluence and freedom of many North

Americans, new options are becoming possible. At this time in history, you and I have multiple claims on our time. We know of many ways to use the resources entrusted to us. Multiethnic and multireligious perspectives abound, revealing varied ways of loving God, self, neighbor and planet.

Sabbath renewal is both the center and the circumference of a Sabbath Economics Covenant. You and I are invited to pay equal attention to the money issues of **debt, spending, having, saving, giving and investing.** We also look at lifestyle issues of **consumption, living green** and **neighboring in solidarity with people on the margins of society.** Each of the following chapters will offer spiritual guidance on a single theme, and tips for creating your own covenant of Sabbath Economics.

OWING:
DEBT AND DEFICIT

The borrower is slave to the lender.

Proverbs 22:7

HAVE AN ALLERGY TO DEBT, an allergic reaction that began long ago. In fact, the prospect of being in debt scares the living daylights out of me. The thought of being enslaved to lenders terrifies me emotionally the way being smothered by a pillow terrified me physically. My brothers thought it was funny to sneak up and press a pillow over my face while I was sleeping. They laughed wildly as I squirmed to get free and squealed in dreadful panic. Debt gives me the same panicky feeling, as if I am being held down against my will and smothered.

At a time when most Americans owe money to multiple lenders, you may wonder why I react so fearfully to debt. *Why, Judith? Why can't you breathe freely when you owe money to others?* For many years, I could not answer that *why* question. The only thing I knew was that I had an irrational fear of debt, with roots so deep that when my husband drove us deep into debt, my terror finally drove me to divorce him.

When most of us think of marital infidelity, our minds go straight to the bedroom. But the secret expenditures that accompany sexual affairs are forms of financial infidelity that also hit the grocery budget and the kids' college funds. Most significantly, secret debts erode trust. California is a community-property state, which means the wife is legally responsible for the husband's debt-load. Judith Newman spoke to my condition in an AARP magazine when she wrote, *Sex isn't the only arena where a partner can betray you. Financial infidelity can also destroy a relationship.*

People may think of money as a rational, concrete topic, but I find it highly emotional and primal: Food and Shelter; Health and Safety; Bondage and Freedom. Marital finances are not *just* about money. Marital relationships inflame emotions whenever partners hold competing values about what money *should* be used for, especially when disagreements get complicated by long-standing issues, such as my fear of being indebted.

TENDING and MENDING DEBT in BELOVED COMMUNITY

Remember Becky and Marian from Chapter One? There is more to the story. In ye olden days, *"all the King's men"* would seize the homes, farms and flocks of early Friends who did not properly toe the early Church of England line, and then summarily toss them into prison. Consequently, Friends have collectively tended and mended each other's debts since those dark days in the 1600s. The first part of Becky's story ended happily when Marian helped arrange an emergency grant to keep the heat on. The frantic mother was able to keep custody of her kids and keep them warm through the harsh Minnesota winter, but she was still deep in debt. Friends formed a Care Committee to support Becky in receiving credit counseling. They also helped her make long-term plans to whittle down her debt-load. (What follows is an idealized model dialogue, please take it as a suggestion for the way positive interventions may unfold:)

"Personal indebtedness is a place where Quaker concern for

the simple life intersects with social justice," said Greg, Clerk of the Care Committee. "I see you, Becky, as a victim of economic injustice. Anyone carrying a balance of a thousand dollars on a credit card from month to month is a slave in bondage to our culture of consumption."

"You've thought about this before," mused Adam.

"Yes, I filed for personal bankruptcy six years ago," said Greg.

"We never knew."

"That's the way I wanted it at the time," replied Greg. "I was embarrassed and too ashamed to admit my mistakes. Now I have a chance to help Becky by sharing some of what I learned the hard way."

"Maybe we could also offer an adult education program for the whole Friends Meeting," suggested Holly. "I'm reading a book on voluntary simplicity, and it is full of good ideas."

"Yes," said Marian. "We have Pendle Hill pamphlets on this subject in the Meeting House Library. They can guide us in protecting more Friends from sliding into debt."

Becky said, "I realize now how my financial problems grew one choice at a time. Thank you for helping when I hit a crisis."

"Your situation can prompt others to live more simply, Becky." Greg spoke kindly. "Being with you through this crisis is showing us ways to take effective preventive action."

"While also addressing the spiritual condition underlying debt," added Adam. "We want to be tender in talking about simplicity, lest it prove a barrier to Friends carrying high debt-loads." "Right," cautioned David. "We don't want to risk having anyone feel blame or shame if they feel they've made a mess of things."

"Let's start by exploring faith and finance in general," added Adam. "That can be our first step, something we can do before people need to ask for help."

Becky sniffled, reached for a tissue and wiped her eyes.

"The poor are not just 'over there.'" Marian's eyes were moist, too. She reached out a hand and touched Becky's arm. "Friends with debts are very near, right here in our Beloved Community. Becky probably isn't the only one."

"Love is the first motion," nodded Greg. "Let's close with a time of silent worship."

A DEBT-ALLERGY STORY

So, Judith, what IS this allergic reaction to debt all about? That question bugged me for a long time after David and I split the sheets and went our separate ways. For years, denial and disassociation kept my debt-allergy hidden away from awareness. Eventually, curiosity coupled with trepidation led me to acknowledge my knee-jerk opposition to debt, and to seek assistance.

I found help in a weekend workshop sponsored by the Ministry of Money, an outreach program of Church of the Savior in Washington, DC. All registrants were asked to prepare for the workshop by writing a Money Autobiography and submitting it to the leaders in advance. Writing my money-story was a novel concept, but I followed the guidelines, did the work, and showed up for the event. There I learned a lot about my financial reactivities — and possibilities — during an intensive weekend under the skilled leadership of its co-directors Dale Stitt and Don McClanen. Don is the founder of Ministry of Money. That Money Autobiography was the first real and productive step toward taking fiscal responsibility for myself. I have repeated the exercise several times since 1988, and benefited from it each and every time.

Don and Dale were men of prayer. They began each session with stillness. They designed Ministry of Money workshops to alternate between speech and silence. The team offered times of teaching followed by times of silent reflection, to record personal insights in our journals. They raised probing questions and gave invitations to share our private responses with one another, in discrete pairs at first. Small-group discussions always included permission to pass. This was a welcome option for introverts like me, because sometimes I was too shaken — or too ashamed — to speak aloud. Money workshops were held at Dayspring Farm, a rural retreat center owned by Church of the Savior. The contemplative rhythm of the weekend included easy access to woodlands, streams and open fields, which grounded me in nature's embrace. Cared-for silence and faith-based leadership gave me plenty of space to get acquainted with my inner money monsters, and to eventually befriend them.

In therapy later, I discovered that my money monster was formed in amniotic fluid when I was still a fetus. Born radiant, like most babies, my future was foreshadowed by foreclosure and parental indebtedness. Mom and Dad's union was founded on a mutual love that kept them together 'til death took Mom in 1984, but their marriage nearly foundered during the first pregnancy (me) when the house they built to welcome me was repossessed by the bank. Mother's milk contained so much sorrow and shame that my baby bones absorbed maternal unworthiness along with the calcium.

JUDITH'S LOVE-MONEY STORY

Fast forward to the first day of college orientation at Pacific University. David flirted with me during lunch in the cafeteria. I was seventeen; he was nineteen. Two nights later, we sat hip-to-hip on the steps of the Carnegie Library and watched the moon rise over the ancient oaks. A bit later he romantically knelt in the moonlight, and asked me to marry him. We shed tender tears of joy, kissed on it, and went back to our respective dorms.

Two years later, we wed. I left my parents' home to live with a man who turned out to be a lot like dear old Dad, plus tall, dark, handsome and more charming. David and I shared many hardships and grand adventures in the course of birthing two sons, adopting one daughter, and raising them the best we knew how. His serial infidelities left bruises on my heart, but he *was* my kids' dad and we *were* living during the Sixties — an era of supposedly *open marriage* — so I did my best to forgive and forget.

After twenty-one years together, however, it became clear that he and I had developed very different financial views and values. David was dedicated to the fierce pursuit of wealth, while I was content with *just enough*. He kept negotiating bigger and bigger loans without my permission or knowledge. When I learned how wildly he was mortgaging and leveraging our modest assets, I was outraged and demanded full disclosure. Once I learned the truth of his (our) indebtedness — which was also legally my indebtedness because California is a community-property state — the amount we owed to lenders exceeded my capacity to bear.

Love and money almost came to blows one night when he grabbed my arm and pushed me against the hearth, but instead of a fistfight, I insisted we go to counseling. By then it was too late. The bond of trust was fractured, and an astute therapist asked if I had already left the marriage emotionally. I had. We divorced with the help of a skillful, restorative (no-fault) lawyer named Les Hait.

I was in mid-life by the time my primal fear of debt heated to the point of volcanic fury at my husband. The twin crises of indebtedness and divorce catapulted me into an urgent search for help. I found ongoing assistance in fiscally wise, spiritually mature guides at Ministry of Money in Washington, DC. I needed a lot of support to embark upon — and stay true to — a fiscally sustainable way of life. It turned out to be radically different from patterns followed by my nearest and dearest. I continued on the path of simplicity and generosity by maintaining close connections with circles of support led by Journey Into Freedom, a non-profit social-change ministry in Portland, Oregon, founded and directed by friends Dale Stitt and Esther Elizabeth. For me, the most trust-worthy dimension of Journey Into Freedom's call to ministry was assisting people like me to seek, find and maintain a life balanced between DOING — the work each of us is called to do in bringing about love and justice in the world — and the work of BEING, which involves continually and consciously deepening relationship with God, self, others and creation.

Contemplative stillness is essential as we let go of longstanding money habits and attitudes. Spiritual guidance is essential as we endeavor to gain financial freedom and integrity. As Dale put it, "Silence is both a call — that which we are to be about — and a gift. Silence gives us the gift of freedom from the daily bombardment of noise. Silence gives us a break from the worldly trap of owning and owing. Silence helps us tune out distraction and find discernment. Silence gives us sacred space in which to relinquish our need for immediate answers, our need to be right, and our need to be in control. It offers space and time for *metanoia*, an opportunity to turn in the opposite direction, away from the dominant consciousness. What better way to hear God than to be in silence with God?"

Silence is the furnace of transformation, wrote Henri Nouwen, *a cauldron in which the straw of our lives can be transmuted into gold.* Silence lets the old pass away and allows the new to be birthed in us. Silence opens us to deeper truths hidden in the heart of God.

Participating in The Great Silence at the end of each *action period* in Haiti gave me annual opportunities to deeply reflect on debt and life after divorce. As I became better acquainted with the Mystery of God, I could finally see the root cause of my allergy to debt. It was imprinted on my young soul when, in unconscious innocence, I somehow came to the unspoken conclusion that money mattered more to my Mom and Dad than I did. Inwardly permeated by parental shame, I came to believe that I too was unworthy. Their intense focus on finances must have convinced my formative self that I was not important enough to deserve full and consciously supportive adult attention.

As a kid, I received consistent messages to keep quiet and be good, because the adults had more important things to do than to pay attention to me. My mission — as I understood it in childhood — was to intuit what others needed and do whatever I could to help them get it. Therefore, love and money got all mixed up. I buried my own wants and needs in order to follow the agendas of loved ones; eventually I even forgot that I had my own wants and needs. By the time I met David, I had adopted the path of *Going Along to Get Along*, which led me into — and eventually out of — a financially-fraught marriage, one in which I was in constant danger of being permanently lost in the valley of the shadow of debt.

BIBLICAL WISDOM

The Hebrew Bible is filled with agonizing accounts of debt-disrupted lives, and dislocated families. Jesus lived in a time of devastating economic hardship. His people were doubly impoverished by the taxes and tolls the Roman occupiers demanded and temple tithes levied by their own priests. Yahweh's people were driven into exodus. As biblical scholar Walter Brueggemann said, *Extreme conditions made the people peculiarly open to the Holy One.*

Where is God when deficit and debt drives us to the edge of our capacity to cope?

Like most modern Jews and Christians, I inherited a God of dominant superiority. Ancient kings claimed that authority came directly from Almighty God. Their power was diminished as it passed down the hierarchy from king to lord to vassal to serf, but the concept of God as Lord left ancient peoples with no choice but to accept the divine rights of "superior" humans. The people lived in fear of the Lord and his rulers because the powers of domination, as always, profited a few and left the rest in debt. *Absolutism was patriarchy's handmaid. Authoritarianism was its stock in trade,* concluded Benedictine Sister Joan Chittister.

In those patriarchal societies, some men ruled, while most women lamented. Five heart-breakingly poetic chapters in the Book of Lamentations convey deep grief as women cry out to an unhearing, uncaring Lord. Daughter Zion pleads for God's attention on behalf of destitute survivors in a destroyed city where their sons have been murdered and their daughters taken into slavery. Abandoned by a cruel, distant Lord, Daughter Zion wails alongside inconsolable widows, anguished mothers, babies dying at the breast and starving children begging for food.

In contrast, the Twenty-third Psalm conveys the Lord as a kindly shepherd whose goodness and mercy endures forever. What do we make of such biblical contradictions? Can both God-images be equally true?

Who is God for you during times of suffering?

Which God comes to your assistance during times of debt, despair and desolation?

My allergy to debt turned out to be a lifesaver because — simply put — debt enslaves. Financial and emotional deficits keep debtors in bondage, and I could not bear a lifelong future of debt. In 2008, my joy in finally finding freedom from the bondage of debt led me to write the first edition of this book, *A Spiritual Guide to Sabbath Economics.* I self-published this, my first book, just before America suffered a painful economic collapse. In 2007, I began to heed God's call to write about finding soulful approaches to owing, owning, spending, having, giving and investing. In 2020, a call from God combined with an interested agent prompted me to revise that twelve-year-old book. This second edition, entitled *Sabbath Economics: A Spiritual Guide to Linking Love with Money,* I hope will introduce spiritual-financial practices to a new generation of readers.

One thing I learned for sure between writing the original book in 2008 and composing this revision in 2020: You and I are able to find the strength to get out of debt, and the commitment to stay out of debt, most reliably when we combine spiritual support structures with social and economic ones. Biblical scholar Walter Brueggemann summed it up best: *Debt asks us to depart from the closely managed world of public survival and to move into the open, frightening, healing world of the Holy One.*

In the New Testament, John's Gospel reveals Jesus as Messiah for all people, with an uncompromising vision of unity in the Beloved Community. Jesus lived in a state of unconditional love and repeatedly broadened the circumference to include more people on the margins. Christians who follow The Way, The Truth and The Life call this Beloved Community.

Don't give in to your distress, said Jesus.
(John 14:1-3, Complete Gospels translation)

When debt drags you down, remember his promise: *You believe in God, then believe in me, too. There are plenty of places in my Father's house. If it weren't true, I would have told you; I'm on my way to make a place ready for you. And if I go to make a place ready for you, I'll return and embrace you. So that where I am, you can be too.*

Now it's your turn. Again.

PRACTICING SELF-INQUIRY
DEBT: OWING

Through all the seasons of my life, where has debt taken me?
  What were the notable lows and highs of my financial life?
    When did hope arise amidst economic tempests and storms?

How have periods of deficit impacted my thoughts? My feelings?
  Does debt make me physically sick?
    Does it cause illness or bodily strain for those I love?

How did family deficits form my views and values?
  Where am I now on the debt/freedom continuum?
    Who is God for me when I don't have enough?

Have I ever gone through the Valley of the Shadow of Debt?
  How did Spirit help me move through a tough situation in the past?
    What did I do then to seek spiritual help?

Do I recall any direct encounters with Love or Light?
  Did I make any deals with this mysterious Power?
    Did I ever feel let down by God?

When did I become aware of learning something valuable from an older person?

Have I ever been surprised to find myself in the role of guide to someone else?

How has a child offered me a fresh perspective?

In workplace or congregation, do I have any sense of the debt burdens others carry?

How can we become aware of others' financial troubles?

How do I acknowledge the essence of goodness in others?

How do I see a spiritual guide (like this book) supporting my journey with love and money?

Which stories or queries can I risk sharing with family, friends, colleagues?

How might digital communication help with money matters?

What kind of life-giving energies emerge when I am able to do the right thing?

DOUBT AND DEBT

Look again at these two words. DouBt and DeBt both have a silent B. My dear editor Michael joked that that silent little b is there solely to disturb. He could be right about that.

DisturBing self-DouBt always shows up when we face personal deBt. Whether you're trying to get a written handle on the debts you owe, or the debts owed to you by others, there is always douBt. But when you face the task of writing about it within the Sabbath Economics circle, you're not doing it alone. The account you want to bring to light is always a collaborative process. While your mind and hand labor to write your story of debt you — yourself — are also being written.

Writing your debt story is the first essential step in linking love and money. The contemplative *bodysoulheartmind* has to become highly receptive in order to receive spiritual guidance from a higher source and pass it along to the conscious mind. DouBt, more than any other aspect of Sabbath Economics, forces us to face our financial limitations, along with our emotional-spiritual deficits. No wonder we resist the task. Writing our deBt story forces us to hear things our ego-defended selves do not want to hear.

Each time we face the hard questions and the blank page, we take another step toward emotional maturity and financial independence. For myself, I sometimes hit the wall when I first try to look deeply into the shadows of my fiscal actions and values. When that happens, I back off for a while. Sabbath rest is an essential part of the love-money process. It is good to take a time-out to think about why we feel stuck, and then pray for help looking at stuff we are not yet willing to see. Then the day comes when the hard questions make sense. My hidden reasons for being stuck become clear. The Light overcomes the darkness, and the hard parts of writing my money-love story get easier.

In the beginning, I hit the wall a dozen times or more. Darkness, for me, is made visible through depression, and the weight of depression keeps me stuck in procrastination. After much practice, I can now write a fresh, updated version of my money-love story without breaking a sweat. Messy first drafts are the hardest part, so don't let the pitfalls of doubt, disgust or disorientation stop you. There comes a time when answers to hard questions rise up from deep within. Without warning, an AHA! floats up through the silence and pops into mind, whole and clear. At that moment, you and your debt story will start to come together as one. The practice of contemplating money will have changed you, just as it changed the old story you've told yourself for far too long. Both you and your debt story can rejoice in becoming more free, more true, and maybe, more grateful.

The story may not turn out the way you thought it would when you began. This is because you shaped a living reality with your intention, your attention and your words. Despite your douBts, your deBt story will find its own shape. It has to. It is a living, breathing story, made fresh every morning by the Source of Love. When you are ready for the truth, it flows through you and out onto the page. The work is never easy, because DouBt is one of the threads of meaning at work within you, and douBt *always* resists hearing and recording what you're being told by your deeper *bodysoulheartmind*.

Sabbath Economics is not a popular practice, so most of your friends and neighbors are not likely to understand what you are doing. Many are not even interested in hearing about it, or why. But novelist Flannery O'Connor would get it. As she humorously predicted: *The truth will set you free, and the truth will make you odd.*

WANTING STUFF

We are what we think. Speak or act with an impure mind and trouble will follow you.

Buddha

A TRUE CRIME STORY

JUDY IS FOURTEEN WHEN THE first Fred Meyer Store opens on Hawthorne Boulevard, just a fifteen-minute walk from her home in Portland. Attracted to the Grand Opening, she strolls alone through the wide aisle of the department store. Shelves are piled high with attractive items.

The girl has fifty cents in the pocket of her denim pedal pushers. Babysitters earn twenty-five cents an hour in 1954. She can't afford to buy much, but the sight of a slender fountain pen fires her desire to acquire. Her hand tickles with desire to hold the maroon pen, elegantly trimmed with gold. Judy picks it up and enjoys its cool elegance. She savors its perfect heft and balance. She puts it down, torn between her small stash of cash and the big price sticker on the lovely pen. A tiny bottle of green ink catches her eye. Desire flares hot again as the young writer imagines her story "Jungle Girl Meets Monkey King" inscribed in emerald green, each word glowing on lined pages of notebook paper.

Judy is an observant child. She notices how far apart the cash registers are located and how the sales clerks are bunched together, chatting among themselves. She notices how little attention the grownups are paying to her. This girl has learned the art of making herself invisible at home, to avoid irritating her short-tempered father. She pretends she is invisible here too, by imagining her body dissolving into mist. She pushes her glasses up, glances from beneath long brown bangs and verifies that not a single clerk is glancing in her direction.

An innocent demeanor comes naturally to Judy. She is, after all, a good Christian girl. Casually, with one hand tucked into a pocket, she picks things up and puts them back on the shelves. She takes another quick glance around. Nobody's watching, so Judy quietly palms the gold-trimmed fountain pen, transfers it from right hand to left and slips it silently into a pocket. That was easy. Feeling bolder now, she moves down the aisle, picks up the bottle of emerald green ink and smoothly transfers it to her other pocket. Folding both hands around her loot, she moves silently on soft-soled sneakers, strolls out the double glass doors and hastily crosses the busy street.

Judy's heart is thundering. She pauses under the marquee of the Baghdad Theatre and pretends to read movie posters, but her mind is too hyper -alert to concentrate on Coming Attractions. Blood pounds behind her eyes as she stares across the street at the store exit door. Is anyone pursuing her? Did a security guard see her pocket the pen and ink?

Wow, it looks like she's in the clear. The thrill of getting away with theft increases as the fear of being apprehended diminishes. She turns away from the scene of the crime and skips down 38th Street, giddy with power, a shoplifter's secret tucked into a corner of her crooked little heart. But the secret is too hot to keep to herself. At home, she proudly shows the loot to her younger brother Jimmy, and brags about the ease and thrill of shoplifting.

Buddha was right. *Act with an impure mind and trouble will follow you.* At fourteen, Judy knew nothing about the tenets of Buddhism, but she'd recently purchased a red-plaster-with-gold-trim statue of Buddha at a second-hand store on Division Street. The Buddha smiled from her bedside table, and she smiled back. Judy tried to copy the lotus-style way of sitting with crossed legs and palms open on her thighs. But the Buddha's gaze bothered her after Jimmy got caught shoplifting. After two policemen brought him home in a cop car. After she worried that he would tell about her crime. After Mom and Dad paid for the softball he stole. After they raised holy hell, grounded Jimmy and confiscated his allowance. After all that, the Buddha's gaze bothered Judy's conscience. Her little brother did not rat on her for coaching him to shoplift, but Buddha did. Buddha's steady, silent eyes made her feel really guilty, so she moved him to the floor of the closet, behind her Sunday School shoes.

Love and money, crime and guilt got all mixed up in my young mind. I knew my actions had harmed my innocent brother, but did not know how to make it right, or where to turn. I was too ashamed to confide in parents or pastor. Too embarrassed to tell friends what I'd done. Too guilty about harsh punishments imposed on Jimmy, while I got away scot-free. Too confused about my brother's decision to protect me from punishment for my secret crime. Too bereft of trustworthy adults to confide in.

As a kid, I had loved going to church and Sunday School, singing hymns and reciting "The Lord's Prayer" in unison with the congregation. I had loved memorizing Bible verses, proud that I could climb up to the lectern during worship and recite scripture to earn my way to summer camp. After getting away with theft, I stopped opening the Bible and stopped attending worship services. Though I did turn up on Sunday evenings for Youth Group, because playing ping-pong with cute boys took my mind off my guilty conscience. Sometimes Al would drive a bunch of us up to Mount Tabor to park in the dark. I liked it when he tuned the car radio to Elvis so I could dance in the street with Al or Chaz, to songs like *Heartbreak Hotel.*

———⁓⌇⦿⌇⦿⌇⦿⌇⦿⌇⦿⌇⌇———

Most of us look for some kind of guidance when life gets overwhelming. Confusion and doubt, guilt and shame. Those combinations jolted me into search-mode at age fourteen, but I had no clear idea what I was searching for. Where could I find a source of wisdom to lead me back onto the path of righteousness? *Who will care about our entanglements with the Ultimate?* asked Carolyn Gratton. Mystery can be terrifying territory. Experienced spiritual guides know the sacred terrain, and are ready to walk with troubled souls through the valley of the shadow of doubt, but it would be decades before I found my way into the ministry of spiritual formation.

Sabbath Economics: A Spiritual Guide to Linking Love with Money is the book I wish I'd had as a teenage shoplifter. I worked after school and Saturdays at the Belmont -Hawthorne branch of the Multnomah County Public Library, and read a lot. But I was well into adulthood before I found any books that led me into connection with *Something More*. It took many years to find my way toward the larger purpose and meaning embodied in the lives and teachings of Jesus and Buddha.

The stories in this chapter are dedicated to my adolescent and young-adult self. Writing them eased my confused mind, soothed my troubled heart and companioned my aching soul. I hope the stories and queries ahead accompany those of you who now search for spiritual guidance. You will encounter a wide variety of probing questions, intended to spark your inner search for spiritual wisdom and support you as you wrestle with the messiness and mystery of love and money.

AN ADULT STORY OF STUFF: THE POVERTY OF TOO MUCH

Waterbed.
Bread machine.
Deep-fat fryer.
Ice-cream maker.
Electric foot massager.
Curling iron.
Hair dryer.

Like many women who came of age in the 1950s, I bought into the idea that the more labor-saving gadgets I owned, the better my life would be. But anyone who has actually cleaned a deep-fat fryer after one failed attempt at homemade donuts knows better. The fabulous things I wanted soon became redundant and redolent with post-purchase melancholy. Nearly every item I bought to make life more varied and more interesting has, in the long run, had the opposite effect.

This was before I read Aristotle, who warned, "It is the nature of desire not to be satisfied, but most humans live only for the gratification of desire."

Midway through the 1980s, friend Penny invited me to join a small group to focus on money. She said she needed female support to grow up financially, and thought maybe I did too. Penny was right, so I said yes. At the time, I was splitting one single interim pastoral position at First Congregational Church with two male colleagues, which meant I was earning only one-third of a modest salary. The other five women who joined the group also worked in various forms of low-paid ministry.

We committed to the radical plan of working our way through mimeographed work-sheets and audiotapes created by Vicki

Robin and Joe Dominguez, co-founders of The New Road Map Foundation in Seattle. The community consisted of nine adults residing in one house, pooling their earnings, keeping costs low and paying the bills by leading workshops titled "Your Money or Your Life." (They went on to publish the book *Your Money of Your Life* in 1992. I recommend it.)

The program developed by the New Road Map pioneers made sense to me because it linked faithful intention with fiscal attention. Their program was not just an idealistic theory: it was a lived reality. They invited me to visit. I got to share a healthy lunch of organic greens, homemade bread, and potato-onion soup with the whole prophetic bunch.

Back in San Francisco, our group of six promised each other to follow practices developed by The New Road Map folks. We did not live together, but did meet twice a month to pray, study, and tell the truth about our financial choices. In between sessions, we counted every penny we earned, spent, saved or gave away.

- We agreed that nobody would miss a meeting unless we had something contagious.
- We reported our failures and successes at tracking income and outgo.
- We listened to each other with mercy.
- We uncovered blind spots and confessed discrepancies between what we said in public and what we actually did with our money.
- We burned away a host of fiscal illusions and delusions.

We gained financial and emotional maturity in Beloved Community.

- We grew in clarity and power over the span of nearly two years.
- We matured enough that each woman left her job in San Francisco and moved on.
- We freed each other to love and serve in more authentic ways, in different places.
- We confirmed that exploring money difficulties, delights, discoveries and dynamics *together, in a safe circle of committed support,* can be a truly combustive combination.

PURGE THE URGE TO SPLURGE
A PLAYFUL PRACTICE from
NEW ROAD MAP FOUNDATION

A Martian anthropologist might conclude that
The Mall is our American place of worship.
Vicki Robin

"Shop-aholism" can be every bit as addictive as workaholism or alcoholism. While consumer moderation may be a virtue, it takes more than virtue to convert most of us from the religion of shopping. Conversion involves willingness, willpower and the imagination to come up with attractive options. You and I can free ourselves from shopaholic dependencies when we set out to discover and rediscover a bunch of free or low-cost activities that yield equal or greater pleasure than "worshipping" at the mall.

Alternate activities can take on whole new levels of meaning when you choose to enjoy them with someone you love. I leave the full range of options to your imagination.

Scan the list below — **Fifty Simple Things to Do Instead of Shopping**

Check the ones that that kindle your imagination
    Add some good ideas of your own
        Mark the most interesting ones with a plus (+) sign or a (*) star
            Identify persons you'd like to ask to join you in each activity
                Mark your **Top Ten** with fluorescent markers
                Post the list on your refrigerator
                Ready, set, GO.

TO PURGE THE URGE TO SPLURGE, I CAN CHOOSE TO

1. Go on a picnic
2. Go for a walk
3. Phone a friend
4. Watch the clouds
5. Take a hike
6. Look at the stars
7. Read a book
8. Teach someone else to read
9. Volunteer someplace
10. Learn to maintain my own car
11. Study another language
12. Learn geography
13. Study nature
14. Go to a nearby botanical garden
15. Go to the zoo

16. Go to a local museum
17. Make music
18. Join a choral group
19. Draw a picture
20. Take photos
21. Write a poem on any topic that comes to mind
22. Write a letter to someone you know
23. Write to a stranger in prison
24. Write to your congress people
25. Write for human rights
26. Write a letter to the editor
27. Dance on the grass until you fall down
28. Join a club
29. Start a club
30. Clean a house
31. Have a garage sale
32. Write a will
33. Write a shopping list
34. Splurge economically at a thrift store
35. Splurge in service by shopping for a shut-in
36. Be a "purchasing agent" for a shelter or hospice
37. Count your money and know exactly how much you earn, spend, give, owe and own
38. Plant seeds in a garden
39. Take flowers or vegetables to someone
40. Bake bread and share a loaf
41. Make soup and give some away
42. Invite guests over to share a meal
43. Practice heart-sharing and listening with total attention.
44. Reach out to someone with tender, non-erotic touch
45. Touch yourself with kindness

46. Make love with care and respect
47. Meditate
48. Chant
49. Visualize world peace
50. Do nothing.

Can you truly do nothing? If so, you are free of shopaholism. Congratulations!

SINKING DOWN
TO THE SEED

This is what the Kingdom of God is like. A man scatters seed on the ground. Night and day, whether he sleeps or gets up, the seed sprouts and grows, though he does not know how.

Mark 4:26-27, NRSV

WHEN I WAS A TEENAGE thief, I developed tics. Rapid blinking and compulsive clutching. Gritting teeth. Lying and inventing cover ups. Avoiding eye contact. Raw nerves and racing pulse. Sullen smugness. Hyperventilating. Snapping under pressure. Picking at cuticles. Sweaty hands.

When I was an acquisitive young wife, I was not nurturing *the seed of God within*. I had bad habits and judgmental attitudes. Jumping to conclusions about others. Mental numbness. Tuning people out. Ignoring the pain of others. Pressed lips. Comparing myself to other people. Blushing when noticed. Jumpiness. Tense muscles. Yelling at kids and our Dalmatian puppy.

Once I began to *sink down to the seed* in contemplative prayer, I enjoyed a greater sense of calm and ease in body and spirit. A growing interest in spirituality. Less need for worldly goods. An aversion to capitalism and partisan politics. A lighter step. Softened facial features. A warmer voice. Unhurried words. Contented sighs. Satisfying new interests. An increased appreciation of my body and what goes into it.

Once upon a visit to the National Museum in Cairo, my attention was captured by a variety of small brown seeds. While most of the visitors *ooohed and aaahed* over the gold items and gems unearthed from King Tut's tomb, my eyes came to rest on a modest glass case. Inside was a simple wooden box divided into many sections. Each section was filled with seeds of different sizes and shapes. Who, I couldn't help but wonder, had buried these seeds alongside King Tut. And why?

The simple shapes and colors of the seeds sharply contrasted with the gleaming treasures that attracted most eyes. I was most curious about the seeds, and asked a museum guard why they were laid to rest alongside the pharaoh. He wrinkled his brow and shook his head, puzzled by my question, since I spoke no Egyptian and his English was limited. When I asked if anyone else knew the story of the seeds, he led me to his boss, who brightened at my question. While the museum director could not explain *why* the seeds had been buried with the jewels, he gladly described what happened after the tomb was excavated. Modern Egyptian biologists decided to plant a handful of ancient seeds in a patch of dirt behind the museum. They watched to see what would happen and — to their great delight — seeds hidden in the dark tomb for three thousand years soon sprouted and brought forth colorful flowers and edible vegetables.

If seeds can remain dormant for millennia and still retain life, what does this fact suggest about the power of God's seed residing in each of us? Isaac Penington, a sixteenth-century Quaker mystic, pondered this profound mystery and came up with wise counsel:

> *Give over thine own willing, give over thine own running, give over thine own desiring to know or be*

anything, and sink down to the seed which God sows in the heart. Let that seed grow in thee, and be in thee and breathe in thee, and act in thee, and thou shalt find by sweet experience that the Lord knows that and loves that and it will seed thine inheritance.

Jesus saw the seed of God in everyone. The rabbi from Nazareth called forth the seed of God in prostitutes, paralytics and tax collectors. He nurtured the seed of God in fishermen and carpenters and mothers, revealing the presence and purpose of love at work in everyday lives.

On my tenth birthday, my mother gave me a tiny mustard seed embedded in a translucent ball of plastic. A slender gold chain around my neck let the seed rest near my heart, reminding me to stay close to Jesus' parable about the tiniest seeds on earth. I still enjoy meditating on the varied Gospel versions of Jesus' parable in Matthew 13:31–32, Mark 4:30–32, Luke 13:18–19 and Thomas 21. Perhaps you will, too.

To summarize the meaning of the mustard seed symbol in Sabbath Economics Spirituality as I practice it, *sinking down to the seed* means slowing down and savoring the sweetness of Sabbath rest. It means tasting the goodness and mercy of Beloved presence, and digesting the fruits of Living Love as they nourish body and soul, heart and mind.

SEED EXPERIENCES: FROM FEAR TO PRAYER

"Thank God for an unhappy childhood!" actress Ellen Burstyn exclaimed to a biographer. I won't repeat her story here, but I do resonate with Burstyn's sentiment.

I was born in Oregon to a family of modest means. They planted plenty of good seeds in me, along with a few weeds. My kin earned their daily bread as farmers, truckers, loggers, electricians, cooks and secretaries. I was a teething infant when bombs fell on Pearl Harbor. I was a toddler when three young uncles donned Air Force uniforms and went overseas. The sirens and sacrifices of World War Two shaped my early childhood. Mom fed us her blue-collar values along with the cod-liver oil, Cream of Wheat, macaroni and cheese.

A broken eardrum kept my father out of the Army. Dad's contribution to the war effort was to rise from his warm bed at three in the morning, walk through the rain to catch a bus to work, load his milk truck with dairy products and deliver fresh milk, cream and cottage cheese to porches all over Portland. Before the Teamsters unionized milkmen, he had no health benefits and no vacations. Dad earned barely enough to keep a roof over our heads. Mom literally kept the home fires burning by cooking on a wood stove in the kitchen and feeding coal to the furnace in the basement. She labored to warm, feed, clothe and guide three children, all of whom arrived together on this Earth in under five years. Given her workload, I think Mom managed the household with remarkable grace, patience and goodwill.

My parents were deeply scarred by The Great Depression. They sacrificed to provide my brothers and me with greater freedom in work and play, love and money than they themselves had enjoyed. I heard more of their love story than their money story. (That was a shameful secret until late in my father's life.) As he approached death, Dad confessed that soon after he married Mom, he overspent by building a house beyond his means. He wanted a snug nest for his family and ordered the contractor to use the very best materials the building trade had to offer in 1939.

Dad's appetite exceeded his bank account. During construction, he added more luxury features like forced-air heating and attic insulation. By the time the house was finished, it cost more than he could pay. He was forced into bankruptcy. Telling me the story sixty years later, Dad's face still flushed with the humiliation of bankruptcy. He still anguished over losing his dream house to repossession by bankers. But, he emphasized, "I only made that mistake once."

I was born early in 1940, soon after their humiliating loss. They brought me home from the maternity ward to a crib in the corner of their bedroom, in a dumpy duplex with a low rent and a leaky roof. My parents struggled to get out of debt all through my early years, and they labored lifelong to stay out of debt by careful planning, scrimping, saving and investing. Their commitment to simple living and thoughtful spending left them with sufficient resources to put two kids through college and later to loan all three kids start-up funds for our first homes and businesses.

My parents sowed in me seeds of working hard so that I too could earn, own, spend, save and give responsibly. Thanks to their choices, I enjoyed enough economic and emotional surplus to feel empathy for people burdened by poverty. Thanks to my generous church-going grandmother, I received sufficient early spiritual guidance to also develop compassion for folks blessed and burdened with wealth. Now it is my work as a writer to pass along my family's legacy of love and money to readers like you — *and to your heirs.*

Forgotten fears from childhood can unconsciously block our desire to meditate or pray during Sabbath hours. Past pain can block present-moment awareness. Pleasant memories can also grab attention when we try to quiet the mind. Nostalgia prefers the past. Nostalgically indulging in memories of comfort or solace dilutes our natural Essence. Focusing attention on the past blocks contact with Sacred Presence, leading to loss of intimacy, responsibility and ecstasy. When we let ourselves get lost in nostalgia, you and I both lose freedom.

The past does have value when we go there intentionally. Upcoming queries can help direct attention toward experiences now behind us. Revisiting the past with curiosity can help us learn from our errors. Writing our money autobiography can free stuck energies and enable us to move past old confusions and mistakes. Humans create meaning by looking back with the light shed by the history of our species, our religious tribe or our loved ones. But escaping into reverie, even during meditation, misses the mark and blocks the "still, small voice" of the Beloved.

Fantasy expresses a preference for living in the future. For all of its attractions and distractions, fantasy also dilutes Essence. When you and I indulge in fantasy during Sabbath quiet, we are likely to miss important insights, in times of sensory intensity. The mysteries of Spirit-infused moments could help to guide our next choice. Focusing properly on the future, however, can be useful to renew our hope, provide a healthier vision and hone direct action. *Escaping* into future fantasies misses the mark; it will surely block access to The Really Real.

SLOWING: SEED QUERIES
for SABBATH TIMES

What is Sabbath like for me these days?
Which animals beckon me to slow down?
Which plants invite me to pay attention?
If I don't yet have real Sabbath time, how might I create it?

When I was young, how did I spend unstructured time?
How did family activities match my innate sense of the sacred?
Or not?
Were there any tensions between my sense of The Holy and theirs?

Looking back for my own early seeds of Essence, what do I notice?
Who nurtured the seed potential within me?
How did emptiness play a part in my coming of age?

How does religion shape my view of Sabbath — for better or for worse?
How does scripture contribute to my perspective, for better or worse?
How do earth, wind, fire and water restore my soul?

In which area of my life do I sense a "*flow*" between my efforts and Holy Spirit?
What happens physically when I am "*in the flow*"?
How does flow guide my thinking process?
Affect my emotions?

Where am I now on the continuum between Doing and Being?
What happens when I encounter 'bad emptiness?'
What sorts of accomplishments have a tight hold on me?

Looking back over my entire life, when was I most fragmented?
When was I most happy and whole?
What was my source of renewal then? Now?

SPENDING:
A SEARCHING
INQUIRY

I am convinced both by faith and experience, that to maintain oneself on the earth is not a hardship but a pastime, if we will live simply and wisely.

Henry David Thoreau

SPIRITUALITY IN ACTION:
A GROWN-UP FIELD TRIP

FIELD TRIPS WERE A GRAND adventure when I was in elementary school. The purpose was educational, of course, but it was great fun to get out of the classroom, climb aboard a big yellow bus and go somewhere interesting. Today, your grown-up mission, should you choose to accept it, is to design and enjoy your own consumer field trip. But not with anyone else this time. This is to be a solo educational experience. The Buddhist Peace Fellowship calls it *Field Trip as Spiritual Practice*.

To prepare for this consumer adventure, first identify your favorite form of shopping. I am entranced by the array of paper goods and pens at Staples. My son Michael's inner compass is set for Fry's Electronics. Daughter Penelope surveys new shoe styles each time she passes through Macy's. Son Ray is totally mesmerized by art supplies wherever they are sold. Friend Sue likes to stock up on household needs at Costco. Neighbor Dean cannot resist buying bargain wines at Trader Joe's.

Ask a few friends where they particularly like to shop.

Tell them what you're up to, and invite them to take their own field trips.

List three of your favorite retail outlets.
Which one is most irresistible today?

Your mission is to go there soon.

Approach this as an opportunity for spiritual practice.

Think of it as walking meditation in a retail store.

What do you see, smell, hear, touch, taste and feel?

Carry a small notebook and pen.

Stroll slowly and mindfully.

Register and record whatever you find pleasing, annoying or tantalizing.

Jot in your notebook I NOTICE THAT I...

Notice and name *whatever* comes to awareness

...sensations... images...emotions... sensations...aversions... questions...inspirations...

Pay exquisite attention to each of your attractions and aversions.

Jot down **key words** to capture your experience

When your retail mindfulness meditation seems complete, find a quiet place to rest and reflect.

Write about the whole field trip.

Describe your experience in detail.

SEARCHING INQUIRY with OTHERS IN A CIRCLE of WARMTH

Does it sound like it might be fun to share your retail field-trip discoveries with friends and family?

SEARCHING INQUIRY is a time-tested practice in many traditions, including Buddhist, Quaker and the many varied twelve-step recovery group circles.

GROUP GUIDELINES: Each person speaks only once, until everyone has had a turn. Refrain from comments, questions, or interruptions of any kind. Leave each speaker free to respond a little or a lot, in whatever way they choose. Reassure participants that they are always free to pass.

SEARCHING INQUIRY is most fruitfully done in small groups, in which participants observe the simple guidelines of posing open-ended reflection questions and then listening respectfully to each person's responses.

Reach deep for what is most true for you....

How can I best describe my favorite store to someone who does not share my affinity?

How can I describe the retail environment to a person who has never been inside it?

What did I buy?

What did I choose not to buy?

What was hardest for me to resist buying?

How am I feeling now about the decisions I made?

What was the "taste" of my craving while I was totally surrounded by favorite stuff?

What did I discover about my own ability to balance between true need and passing desire?

Where is the beginning of my own slippery slope?

When and how do I sense myself sliding from desire to greed?

What new promptings or choices am I aware of since my field trip?

SHEDDING:
LETTING GO

HOW MUCH WILL I MISS THIS IN A CRISIS?

THE GOOD NEWS IS THAT one small beloved community of committed women set me on the path toward financial freedom. The bad news is that my home cupboards and closets still kept filling up. I claimed to be simplifying, so I refused, on principle, to rent a storage locker. Accumulate or eliminate: that became the standard to live by. Seeking ways to shed more stuff led me to "The Absence Test" devised by London executive Jeremy Bullmore. He posed a great question: *How much would I miss this item in a crisis?*

Today, as I write, ash from nearby wildfires sifts past my Southern California windows. If ordered to evacuate, how much would I miss this mirror or that vase? This book or that lamp? On a scale of 1 to 100, how vital would my electric rice cooker be in a time of fire, flood or earthquake? Bare necessities and simple pleasures rarely disappoint. Still, stuff tends to pile up.

When do I accumulate and when do I eliminate?
Once a year I apply *The Usefulness Factor:*

Have I worn this jacket within the past year?
    No? OK, out it goes to someone who needs
    a jacket.

Have I baked any food in this Pyrex dish during the year?

Nope. Off it goes to the community rummage sale.

Am I likely to use my cross-country skis, poles and boots within the next year?

Here's where honesty can arm-wrestle with fantasy.

- No, I have not gone cross-country skiing for the past five years.
- Yes, I have fudged on the annual review a few times.

OK. Sigh. It really is time to give away my ski stuff. If I want to go cross-country skiing some fine winter day, I can always rent the equipment.

No, I haven't been backpacking lately either, but I'm not ready to let go of the vision that I might. Not yet. Sometimes I bend my own Usefulness rule. I tuck my backpack gear back into the closet. I might still hit the trail some fine day. God only knows…

WHAT ARE YOU CARRYING? A SPIRITUAL PRACTICE

Jesus said: The Father's imperial rule is like a woman who was carrying a jar full of meal. While she was walking along a distant road, the handle of the jar broke and the meal spilled behind her along the road. She didn't know it; she hadn't noticed a problem. When she reached her house, she put the jar down and discovered it was empty.

Gospel of Thomas 97:1-4

What are you carrying?
>   Where are you walking?

What do you think you already have a handle on?
>   How might it be broken, though you haven't
>   yet noticed?

When have you put down a responsibility, only to discover that it had already been empty of meaning for a while, before you noticed the problem?

Have you made any startling discoveries upon reaching your true home?

When do you long for emptiness?
>   Where, how, and with whom do you find it?

Sabbath emptiness comes in two forms: scary and sacred. Scary emptiness can bring up unease or a sense of dread. Unstructured time can leave us feeling bad. Deficient. Not-okay with ourselves. Poking around in the muck of inner emptiness can reveal insides that are not empty after all. My gut may be full of old hurts. Memories of shame. Feelings of neglect. Painful childhood pains. Adult failures and regrets. The scolding voice of emptiness may say:

"Uh-oh. I haven't accomplished enough.
>   I haven't accumulated enough.
>   I'm afraid I am not enough."

ESTHER ELIZABETH'S STORY

"As a child of the Christian tradition, I wrestle with demons that have been implanted in my head about how God wants more of me and expects me to do more, to feed more hungry people and work harder for justice, to visit more people in prison, and take care of more neighbors. The list is endless. The Christian message I embodied (which is not the message I now believe) was clear — "In God's eyes, I will always have to be something more than I am and do more than I am doing"."

"As a child of North American culture, it is hard for me to be at peace with who I am or what I have. I live in an ever-restless society that seeks happiness through accomplishing and accumulating. This notion is a lie. And the lie holds us in bondage. When I feel flawed, deficient, and not good enough, I tend to look at others through this same lens. It makes me feel they want more of me than I'm able or willing to offer."

"I want to be resurrected, brought back from the dead. I want to live life fully, believing in my gut that I am beloved, that I am made in the image of God, that even as I continue to grow into wholeness, I am — right now, in each and every moment — enough. The God I know is a liberating God who accepts me as I am. If the derelicts and ragamuffins that Jesus hung out with were good enough for Jesus, then so am I."

"I am enough when grounded in my relationship with God. I am enough when I turn my will over to the care of God as I understand God. I am enough when I get my ego out of the way and allow the Spirit of Love to move through me. In this place of enough-ness, I experience a deep sense of well-being and can reside in the truth that *All will be well, and all will be well, and all manner of thing shall be well.*" (Julian of Norwich)"

ESTHER ELIZABETH'S POEM

To celebrate being enough and having enough, she composed words I hear as a prayer:

DEMONS

It is not enough said her dad to
Win the sports tournament
Take first place in the speech contest
You must become
The boy I wanted

It is not enough said her mother to
Graduate with honors
You must visit your dying grandmother
And fulfill the dreams I had for myself

It is not enough said her husband to
Give up your identity
You must be the managing director
Of my domain

It is not enough said her child
That you make cookies for school functions
And be a soccer mom
You must give up your life
And tend to mine

It is not enough said her minister
That you give your life to Jesus
You must teach Sunday School classes

Serve on all the committees
And organize the food bank

It is not enough "they" said
It is not enough
You are not enough
We need more of you

She became very very tired
As the demons in her head
Continued to claim her life
And dry rot her soul

One day
While sitting under a tree
These words were whispered
In her being
It is all a lie

She stood up
And began twirling around and around
While demons left
And angels sang
She kept on dancing
And
As her soul was restored
She claimed her life.

LISTENING INWARDLY

Does this offend you?

John 6:61

THE PRACTICE OF POSING SHARPLY pointed questions goes back to the Hebrew prophets. Jesus posed hard questions too, with disciples, peasants and power brokers alike. Queries have also been central to Quakers since the 1600s. The still-evolving set of queries in use today is based on Friends' historic and current practices and testimonies. For members of The Religious Society of Friends — along with generations of mystics and saints from all religious traditions — direct personal experience with the Source of Love provides dependable spiritual guidance, even more than book knowledge or church knowledge. Questions, not answers, guide Friends — individually and corporately — to practice continual self-reflection and self-examination.

To question IS the answer. I do not know who first said that, but the phrase galvanized me one morning during the Sixties when I spotted it on a bumper sticker, on a car in the Unitarian Fellowship parking lot. I have tested the truth of this phrase for forty years, and have found that a proper interrogation of the question itself can consistently provide more useful answers than any of the creeds and dogmas proclaimed by religious authorities.

My first spiritual director demonstrated the art of curious questioning when she would pause and ask things like *What image do you see when you feel lonely? What happens in your throat when you pray to God?* Well-crafted questions still companion me in moving from outmoded secular values to lifegiving sacred practices with love and money.

I've learned to steer clear of people who ask loaded questions that start out, *Don't you think you should...* Jesus asked open questions, not loaded ones. *Don't you think you should* comes tainted with opinions, judgments and unrequested advice. Avoid them. On the other hand, open, curious questions point the way toward growth by encouraging us to evaluate our options, our actions and our decisions. Curious questions raise awareness, clarify confusions, invite self-awareness and lift up social concerns. They enliven us and may affirm our commitment to shed old habits and move forward with more generous approaches to love and money. Open, curious questions are often uplifting and empowering. I find it great fun to practice the art of collecting and creating them. Perhaps you will, too.

As the rabbi from Nazareth demonstrated, people get upset when confronted with ideas they do not readily understand. *Does this offend you?* he asked the disciples (John 6:61 NRSV). Many followers bailed out after hearing him teach on the power of resurrection through his body and blood, *So Jesus asked the twelve, 'Do you also wish to go away?* (John 6:67)

Challenging questions can often create dynamic tension in our spiritual lives, too, especially when they point out discrepancies between our actions and beliefs, or illuminate how far we have strayed from our deepest values in the ways we are handling love and money. You and I can always turn and walk away from such tough questions, as many of Jesus' early followers did — or we can choose to walk alongside them, as the twelve disciples did.

In working your way through this spiritual guide, I recommend strolling for a while beside the discomforting questions — those you encounter here and elsewhere — rather than hurrying into premature answers.

TWENTY QUESTIONS, REVISTED

Where am I now?
Where am I in this moment, in relationship to the twenty questions
I first encountered at the beginning of this guide?

What have I noticed about myself so far?
What privileges and possibilities occur to me?

What am I most grateful for in these pages, so far?
Least grateful?

As I read the *Prelude,* which notions rankled me?
Which ideas and images resonated with mine?
What put me off?
What pulled me in?

What happened inwardly as I read *Sabbath — Slowing?*
What role does silence, stillness and solitude play in my spiritual life?
Which of the Sabbath suggestions continue to annoy me?
Which practices refresh my body, soul, heart and mind?

As I read *Debt/Owing,* what emotional reactions did I notice arising in me?
What do I hide from others?
How do I let others help me sort out my financial problems?
How does the concept of Beloved Community fit for me?

As I read *Stuff/Wanting,* how did I react mentally?
What did I argue with?
What did I agree with?
Who assists me in figuring out how to handle guilt?

At this point in the book, what personal questions about love and money are occurring to you?

PAUSING WITH PRESENCE

God is beyond all our words because God is beyond all our thoughts. If we only deal with God in words, then essentially we have removed ourselves from God. Silence is an introduction to the infinite, and all words are finite.
Father Thomas Keating, Trappist Monk

Perhaps you sense the power of Presence pulsing through these pages. I hope so. I hope you sense the powerful life-force flowing from Holy Source through the words on these pages and into your consciousness. I hope you feel Great Belovedness flowing in your veins and infusing your love-money work. I hope you follow living threads of connection between the visible realm of daily life and the imaginal realm of unity with Sacred Presence, becoming ever more firmly rooted and grounded in Beloved Community. In eight decades of taking risks and making mistakes, I have become totally convinced that being present to both self and the Sacred is more vital than anything else in exploring the delicate issues intertwining love with money. Presence is more essential than any methods or queries that I, or any other author, can devise. Perhaps this is what the novelist Frank Herbert meant when he said, *The mystery of life is not a problem to be solved, but a reality to experience.* And maybe it is what poet Robert Frost meant when he wrote, *These are not monologues, but my part in the conversation.*

You, dear reader, have vital insights to contribute to the conversation.

> If any of these queries make you bark *"I don't know, dammit!"* please close the book.
> Take a deep breath.
> Push the book away from you, out of sight.
> Take three more deep breaths.
> Stand up and shake off any tension in your hands, arms and legs.
> Inhale deeply through your nose.
> Fill your lungs with air. Fill up all the way to your belly button.
> Pause for a moment in complete fullness.
> The Presence of Love accompanies you here in fullness.
> Exhale fully through your mouth. Empty out every ounce of air.
> Pause for a moment in total emptiness.

The Presence of Love accompanies you when you
are empty.

Pause with Presence — and notice what else is
happening in your body.
Sensations of tightness, jumpiness or itchiness are
signals to slow down.
Inhale through your nose, pause, then exhale
through your mouth.
Say hello to whatever is going on within you.
Take your time.
Keep breathing with Presence.
Keep noticing and naming whatever you notice
happening within you.
This is sacred work.
No judgment. No shame. No blame.
Keep doing Sabbath practice, right in the midst
of each uneasy moment.

*If a pointed question poked too hard, reframe it as a
friendly suggestion.*
For example, did the question W*here are you?* cause
you to growl, *"I have no idea!"*
Imagine a spiritual guide gently asking you to
describe the quality of that growl...
Sense a kind companion listening with you for the
message of the growl...
Where are you now?

The path ahead is paved with queries.
Some may poke or pinch.
Some may hug or kiss.

Stay alert.
Some questions have your name on them.
Some don't.
Skip those.
Approach these questions with care.
Embrace one, if you dare.
Bear it gently, but persistently.
When you feel ready,
delve into it with daring and deliberation.

Keep one key question to keep in mind, however:
Am I committed to seeing what love can do?

There will always be unanswered questions in our spiritual and financial lives, and more room to grow. Allow unresolved questions and unsatisfied desires to take you where they will, maybe even deep to the core, to the inward dwelling place of your wise inner guide.

SABBATH: SLOWING AND FLOWING

In which area of my life do I sense a "*flow*" between my efforts and Spirit?
What happens physically when I'm "*in the flow*"?
How does flow guide my thinking process?
How does *flow* affect my emotions?

What is Sabbath like for me these days?
Which animals beckon me to slow down?
Which plants invite me to pay attention?

If I don't have enough real Sabbath time, what might I do to create it?

How did I spend unstructured time when I was young?
How did family activities match my innate sense of the sacred?
Were there tensions between my ideas of The Holy and theirs?

Looking back for my own early seeds of Essence, what do I see?
Who nurtured the seed potential within me?
How did emptiness play into my coming of age?

How does religion shape my view of Sabbath — for better or for worse?
How does scripture contribute to my perspective, for better or worse?
How do earth, wind, fire and water restore my soul?

Where am I now on the continuum between Doing and Being?
What happens when I encounter 'bad emptiness'?
What sorts of accomplishments have a tight hold on me?

Looking back over my entire life, when was I most fragmented?
When was I most happy and whole?
What was my source of renewal then? Now?

TENDING REGRETS, TUNING HEARTS

Will you ever bring a better gift for the world than the breathing respect you carry wherever you go right now?

-William Stafford

W HEN MY FATHER DIED, I inherited more than money. I also inherited regrets.

Dad was a gambling man, driven to pit gut instincts against the stock market. He practiced creative frugality in everyday life, wound up with more money than he could spend, and left a legacy for his descendants. I inherited more money than I could ever earn as a pastor, and much more money than I could ever sock away in a personal IRA.

In addition to assets, I inherited a tangle of emotions mixed with sibling rivalry. In the wake of our father's death, I inherited grief and distrust, sorrow and suspicion. This volatile combination pushed me into disrespecting my youngest brother by saying and doing things I now deeply regret.

I regret the way I chose to ignore my brother's professional guidance.

I regret suspecting Bob of wielding his CPA *know-how* to seize power over Jim and me.

Jim shared my suspicion that Bob wanted full control over Dad's estate. Over us.

I regret the way Jim and I broke the family trust, crafted so carefully by Bob and Dad.

I regret taking sides with one brother to gang up on the other, an awful childhood pattern.

The words of William Stafford (above) did not come to me back when I needed them. Stafford was appointed the Poet Laureate of Oregon, where parents, brothers and I all grew up. But our family did not read poetry. I regret not breathing respect for Bob at the time of Dad's death. We all would have benefited from embodying greater respect, especially the youngest boy in the family. Jim and I did not show respect for Bob when we were kids, either. We played tricks on him. We left him out of childhood games, left him behind on hikes, and kept secrets from him.

Bob inherited Dad's fascination with money. He earned a BA in accounting and further credentials as a Certified Financial Planner. He managed funds for the University of Oregon, and put his knowledge to work in managing our father's money as well as theirs. He developed monetary skills far beyond mine. I regret failing to respect Bob's fiscal acumen.

A plumbing metaphor might describe what happened between us in 1999, a few months after dad's funeral. Imagine the pipes that bring water into your home. When all sections of pipe are aligned and correctly joined, water flows freely. The flow is blocked if any part of the pipe has a kink, or if the plumber laid it down askew. Even if the pipes were installed correctly, whenever the temperature drops below freezing and stays there for a while, the pipes may even burst. Storms of grief and loss combined with sibling rivalry iced the pipes that connected my heart and brain. The flow of love was blocked. My heart iced up and so I broke our family trust in more ways than one.

Regret comes from the old French word *regreter.*
It translates as *one who bewails the dead.*

Dad is dead. Jim is dead. I bewail both of them.
Bob is not dead, but he does not respond to my
calls and letters.
He did call once, when his daughter Sigrid was
hospitalized in serious condition.
He did write one letter of condolence, last year
after my son Ray died. These are the only forms
of contact my brother has initiated with me in
twenty-plus years.

I regret my part in breaking the pipe that once
connected us.
I regret that the breakage cannot be undone.
I regret our years of estrangement.
I regret not being able to share these closing years
with my one surviving brother.

Looking back across two decades of separation, I can see my
icy heart as a spiritual disability. Perhaps Bob also suffers from
the same spiritual disability? Maybe that kept him from joining
us in the closing days of our father's life.

Jim and I kept vigil in ICU for four days.
We saw Dad's face and body twist in pain.
We heard his last words. *I'm getting out of this
goddamn place. I'm going HOME!*
We saw him grab my forearm to hoist his body
up from the bed.

115

We saw his spine arch, his chin tilt up, and his
eyes open wide.
We saw Dad's wrinkled, stubbly face transformed
by love and wonder.
Jim and I looked up too, toward the source of glory
our father had glimpsed.
All we saw was the hospital ceiling.

Our father saw Something More in his passing
moments.
His dying vision extended far beyond what our
human eyes could see.
His last breath carried us into a state of union, into
a state of Oneness too large for words.
Bob missed these transformative moments with
Dad.
I regret that too.

TUNING THE HEART

*It is the attainment of harmony that is called heaven,
and the lack of it is termed hell. The harmony of life
can be learned in the same way as the harmony of
music. With every step forward in evolution, there
comes a change in voice. Every experience in life is an
initiation… Any pain or suffering is a preparation.
Just as one must first tune a violin to play it, so the
heart must be tuned in order to express wisdom.*
- Hazrat Inayat Khan

Dad grasped my forearm with both hands in his last desperate attempt to hoist his frail body from the bed. He intended to get out of that hospital and *go HOME*. His death grip electrified me. It animated Something More within me, though I had no words to describe what that might be. It took years to metabolize the mystery. Now I understand my father's legacy as something far greater than the stock and bond earnings he accumulated during a boom economy. Bob carefully crafted our father's surplus funds into a family partnership trust, but in the last moments of his life, Dad gave me Something More.

> I received a direct jolt of glorious, painful energy
> from my father's parting touch.
> His death grip on my arm tuned my heart to
> something too deep for words.
> It left me startled, confused and grieving, on the
> threshold of transformation.

> Jim witnessed Dad's radiance from the other side
> of the bed.
> It changed him, too.
> We both felt the joy and heard the hum of Oneness
> that unites all beings.
> I regret that Bob was not there to share this
> indescribable experience.

> I regret the spiritual disability that iced my heart.
> Dad intended to keep his three kids in relationship
> through a legal family partnership.
> I regret breaking his trust.

MENDING REGRETS through CONTEMPLATIVE WRITING

In your journal, describe in detail one action you regret taking, or not taking.

- Imagine this regret as an animal that has taken up residence in your attic.
- What kind of noise does it make in the night?
- How much space does this creature take up in your memory bank?
- How do you feel when you hear it growl or thrash about?
- What other emotions does it kick up in your heart?

Lament comes for a reason. It has its season.

- How have the seasons changed since the hurtful event?
- What might you do now to tend and mend this old regret?
- What might you do to release the weight of it?

PAIRED SHARING

In conversation with a friend, describe someone with whom you have tangled emotions. Explore together how you might separate your feelings from the feelings of the other.

Try this:

> Place two blank pages side by side on a desk.
> Make a list of your feelings on one page.
> Make a list of his or her feelings on the other.
>
> Set it aside for a week.
> Let love lead the way into Sabbath rest.
>
> Revisit your list.
> What do you notice?
> (Tell your friend.)

PAUSING

Everything that slows us down and forces patience,
everything that sets us back into the slow cycles of
nature, is a help when we need to learn to pause.

May Sarton

WHAT WOULD IT BE LIKE to intentionally stop rushing around — just for two minutes?

What would it be like to pause right now and notice what is going on inwardly?

When we pause, we simply discontinue whatever we were doing — thinking, eating, talking, writing, planning, worrying, wanting — in order to become wholeheartedly present. Pausing invites us to be fully attentive and, often, physically still. Learning to pause is a key step in the practice of seeking and finding inner guidance when we are faced with choices about love and money.

To pause is to suspend activity. To pause is to — temporarily — stop moving toward a desire, a person, a goal or an excuse. We can pause in the midst of anything, and our pause can last for an instant, an hour or an entire season of life. On sabbatical, we step away from calendar, clock, and everyday responsibilities for an extended period. In a conversation, we pause for a moment, let go of what we were about to say and choose to fully listen to the other person. In a moment of shock, the gut stops. When awe moves the heart, the breath stops. When we sit down to meditate, mental activity slows down.

A pause is, by nature, time-limited. We resume our activities afterward, with increased attentiveness and greater ability to make wise choices. In the pause before we sink teeth into a chocolate bar, for instance, we might sense a foreground tingle of anticipation, and perhaps a background cloud of self-judgment. We may eat it all, or choose to fully savor only one bite. After the pause, we may also decide to skip the calories and go for a run instead. Pausing reminds us that we always have a choice.

When we're in a fit of anger, or overheated by lust for someone or something, the last thing we want to do is pause, yet these are the times we most need a time-out. Pausing disrupts habit-driven behaviors and opens us to fresh, creative ways of responding to our wants and fears. Pausing develops our inner capacities to stop running from our experience, and stop hiding our mistakes. Love and money habits are particularly persistent. Pausing helps us weigh the options and make better choices. Over time, pausing teaches us that it is safe to trust our inward spiritual guide.

DAD'S LONG PAUSE

Living within an aging body and without a driver's license was a trial for dad. This combination imposed a long and unchosen pause upon my formerly-active father. "They used to call me a *firecracker*," he boasted in old age, "all 6 foot 4 inches of me."

"Except, Dad," I wanted to interrupt, "a firecracker explodes only once, while you kept exploding over and over."

That was when something in me said *pause*. In that pause, I decided to keep my opinions to myself. Taking a pause gave me space to choose to listen instead of expounding or exploding.

My father was not one to compare himself to literary figures like Henry David Thoreau, who deliberately chose a very long pause on Walden Pond. No, dad's confinement on the shore of Rock Creek Reservoir was unbidden. Age, illness and two broken hips stripped him down to the essentials. And while my dad never spoke of his life in terms of introspection, I chose to interpret it in that way. I watched him spend his final decade in pause-mode, which happens when physical limitations constrict a person to the footpath of home. He did have a choice. My *firecracker* dad might have chosen to resist reality and fight against it. But James Leo Wright chose to accept his situation, if not with grace, then certainly with forbearance.

He had, after all, chosen his final dwelling place. Many decades earlier, he had chosen to fish and camp alone on this very site, beneath these sturdy pines. My dad never used words like meditation or prayer, but every time he got two days off from work, he headed for the mountains to go fishing. It was during these long, silent pauses outdoors, communing only with nature, that he first saw visions of living on this very lakeshore.

In the Fifties, the Native American couple living on this part of the shore granted him permission to fish in their waters.

In the Sixties, when the land was purchased from tribal leaders and developed into the privately-financed Sportsman's Park, Jim was first in line to put down money on two lakefront lots with great views. I helped my parents pack up stuff from their three-story home in Portland, downsize and move to Dad's dream-place.

In the early Eighties, he paid contractors to construct a well-designed prefab house on the edge of the lake. I was there to help them move in.

They had less than two years together in that house before Mom died.

Over the next fourteen years, he created his sanctuary in Oregon, the land of his birth. Dad dwelled alone on the shore of a small lake. It was not Walden, but it was wild and quiet and beautiful. He found his place of repose on the southeastern shoulder of Mt. Hood, on the edge of this reservoir formed by an earthen dam, on a parcel of land surrounded by National Forest. He had exercised his freedom to choose while he was strong and agile, and used this freedom to craft the home that sheltered him in later years.

He even chose his next-door neighbor, a freedom not granted to many of us. In Jerry Fisher, dad saw a man dedicated to helping others, so he sold the adjacent lot to Jerry and loaned the money to finance construction of his house. The investment paid off. As my father aged, it was Jerry who offered steady neighborly companionship, brought in groceries and cut firewood for the Earth stove. And it was Jerry who saved Jim from dying alone in a cold house. Early one morning in late October 1998, the next-door neighbor saw no smoke coming from dad's chimney. He used his key to enter, and found my dad unconscious, but still breathing. Jerry called an ambulance and accompanied him sixty miles to the hospital in The Dalles. The heart attack weakened Jim, but Jerry's attentiveness extended my father's life for four days, long enough for loved ones to gather around him. Our goodbyes were tender. We exchanged memories and appreciations. For the first time, my father said, "I love you." My brother Jim and I stood beside him at the end, holding him in love as his heart seized. We watched his eyes widen, heard his breath catch in his throat, then stop. We beheld his face as it expressed pure awe.

Dad's death was suffused with amazing grace. The power of his passing forever marked me. I can't help but ponder what he experienced at the last. From where we stood, it certainly looked as if he was greeted by glory.

Jim lived for three years after the Oregon DMV cancelled his driver's license. It was a huge loss for him, not being able to run errands, explore back roads or drive to Gresham to visit Glady, his widowed lady-friend. Jim had been the quintessential driver. He earned his living as a Teamster. Driving was central to his identity. It humbled him to have to depend on me to drive him around. Deprived of car keys, Jim was forced to find a new form of freedom.

Did his fourteen-year pause provide moment-by-moment instruction on how to spend his closing years of confinement?

Did thousands of hours of solitude prepare a proud "firecracker" to go home to Love?

Solitude, though silent, is not without voice. Nature came calling each day. From his recliner beside the sliding glass door, Jim heard sparrows squabbling, watched eagles mating in mid-air above the lake, and followed the path of wild geese with his binoculars as they winged south in autumn and north in springtime.

Perhaps his best company was the weather. Better than any movie, the movement of sun, clouds and stars continually played across the wide sky visible from his recliner. Each hour of each day offered different angles and degrees of light. Wind, clouds, sun, rain and snow formed patterns of constant change in the mountains of Oregon. Barometer and thermometer became as vital to Jim as coffee and Pepsi. Without people in the house to prompt emotional reactions, his moods rose and fell along with changes in rainfall, temperature and barometric pressure.

As Thoreau recorded his delight in the freedom of an extended pause at Walden, Jim became the author of his own constricted life on Rock Creek Reservoir. He was not much of a writer, apart from the daily discipline of recording the rise and fall of stocks that interested him. After Mildred died, however, my dad adopted her practice of sending cards to dear ones to celebrate our birthdays and Christmas. His handwritten notes were always simple, sometimes only *Love, Dad*.

It was enough.

PART THREE

FLUIDITY

FRIENDS OF GOD, AND PROPHETS

In every generation, she (Wisdom) passes into holy souls, and makes them friends of God, and prophets.
The Book of Wisdom 7:27

ROGER'S STORY

"THE POOR OF HAITI ARE *the suffering strong*," Father Roger Desir told me during a meal at his home in 1991. "Serving my people is my life and my faith."

As a unique way of serving his people, Roger told of laboring for decades to translate the Bible into the Creole language. Creole, a blend of native Arawak Indian and French, is the native language of the Haitian people. The French language was imposed as the 'national tongue' when France conquered Haiti in 1697. Since then, all official matters of government, business, religion and education are conducted in French. Most people never mastered the language, mainly because Haiti lacks a public school system. French is taught in private schools, but school fees are beyond the means of most citizens. Roger's family was wealthy enough to pay for his education, but he was pained by his privilege, aware that the majority of his Haitian brothers and sisters could not read and lacked access to the Holy Bible.

As a young friend of God, Roger anguished over his country's systemic inequalities, and prayed fervently for guidance. His prayers were answered when he was a young priest serving the Cathedral of the Holy Trinity in Port-au-Prince. Father Desir clearly heard God's call to strengthen the souls of *the suffering strong* by giving them direct access to scripture. He doubted that he had what it took to translate the entire Bible into Creole at first, but the now legendary scholar-activist got to work on it. He had a full schedule of priestly duties, but set about this daunting task in his spare time. He labored and grew weary, but persisted. Bending over his desk, engrossed in translation, he ignored his aching back and burning eyes.

Roger would get so caught up in the translation work that he only stopped when his wife summoned him to meals. Their sons grew up and left home. He stayed true to his call, and had translated as far as The Book of Hebrews when his wife was diagnosed with cancer. He kept vigil at her bedside, wept at her death, and returned to his task. At the finish line, he thanked God for the fortitude to make it to the closing words of the Book of Revelation:

The grace of the Lord Jesus be with all the saints. Amen.

QUESTIONS FOR REFLECTION AND DISCUSSION

- Do you know someone who serves *the suffering strong* here or abroad?
- What questions might you want to ask him or her?
- What kind of guidance might you seek from an open conversation?
- Who else do you see paying a high price to be a *friend of God, and prophet?*
- How do his or her words and actions illuminate unity with the Beloved?

ACCEPTING THE COST

The prophetic voice is our common call in Christ.
Patrick Carroll, S.J

Being prophetic can be costly, but committed friends of God are willing to pay the price. Roger Desir's story has a happy ending, whereas many prophets suffered scorn and rebuke, even death on a cross or a pyre.

When Saint Francis proclaimed unity with God, and the animals and birds, his wildly prophetic words and actions made him the laughingstock of his hometown.

When colonial Quaker Mary Dyar insisted upon publicly proclaiming the power of unity with God, she was decried as a heretic, imprisoned and publicly hanged on the Boston Common.

When Catholic activist Dorothy Day showed unconditional love for neighbors who were misfits, and solicited money to feed and shelter them, she was mocked as a fool.

Gandhi was assassinated for his public prophecies. So was Martin Luther King, Jr.

Contemplative practitioners of Sabbath Economics are likely to be reluctant prophets, and for good reason. You and I may eagerly want to share the treasures we have discovered in making contemplative-based choices about love and money, only to find that speaking publicly about it alienates our dearly beloveds. Although deeply convinced of the economic and racial wrongs that need to be made right, we may be shy to speak out. Most of us want to be more than an angry voice crying in the wilderness. Know that we can be. What it takes is to remember that our words and actions are rooted in unity with the Beloved and urged on by the voice of Christ. When prayerful prophets become deeply rooted and grounded as friends of God, our Great Creator inspires us to be creative in finding the right forms of prophecy.

QUESTIONS FOR REFLECTION AND DISCUSSION

- Who or what first led you to assume that only *the specially chosen* are called to be friends of God, and prophets?
- If this viewpoint came from sacred scriptures, what might happen if you went back to those texts and reread them with a fresh and renewed curiosity?
- How do you see *friends of God* expressing creativity with love and money?

WHERE IS SPIRITUAL GUIDANCE IN ALL THIS?

I once was blind, but now I see...

Amazing Grace

Soul work becomes essential when we see something to which we have been blind, and the sight of it shatters our self-image. We often want to turn away, to wish we had not seen it. My eyes leaked constant tears the first few days I was in Port-au-Prince. Tears blurred my vision and softened the edges when I was presented with all that evidence of anguishing poverty, but once seen I could never un-see the misery suffered by countless Haitian women, men and children. At first, I just wanted those feelings of helpless despair and agonizing guilt to go away.

The God of Love saw me discomforted and accompanied me through chaotic emotions by encircling me with people of faith who slowly helped me integrate stuff. Disruptive feelings are part of spiritual transformation. Waking up to my white privilege was not as much fun as viewing Haiti from the safe distance of a deck chair on a Caribbean cruise ship, as so many Americans have chosen to do. The disruptive discomfort of sleeping on banana leaves in a hut buzzing with hungry mosquitos awakened something in me that would never have come to light in a white-sheeted bunk aboard a luxury liner.

My author-self had been hidden behind my good-girl mask for half a century. The anguish I experienced in Haiti awakened creativity in me, and being a *friend of God* infused me with the capacity to write and publish books on topics that matter.

Shattering the mask also set me free to be more deeply present to those who come to me for spiritual companionship. I do not introduce topics of Sabbath Economics or white privilege into my sessions with spiritual direction clients. To do so would be to impose my agenda on our time together. However, experience and reflection has prepared me in case someone does raise issues of love or money, or even racism or classism. If anyone feels led to go beyond being *friends of God* to take on the challenges of becoming a *prophet,* I have greater capacity to walk this path with them than I had before my heart was broken open to the truth of white privilege in Haiti.

As a seasoned spiritual director, I am honored each time a troubled soul chooses to confide in me. For forty -plus years, I have been blessed to witness many unique forms of commitment to the path of love and justice. When people entrust me to hear struggles and insights, pains and growth, questions and confusions, I see ordinary souls visibly becoming greater *friends of God, and prophets.*

The journey with Sabbath Economics parallels the journey of soul work, and neither of these are do-it-yourself projects. When grace breaks in, we are given eyes to see injustices to which we were formerly blind. You and I need help in order to stay true to this conversion process, whether it begins suddenly — as mine did in Haiti — or more gradually. Transformation in matters of love and money requires spiritual guidance and support. As our values change, we will surely find ourselves called to do things differently, especially if some our most vital relationships dissolve or deepen.

Sister Mary Ann Scofield, a founder of Spiritual Directors International, sums it up:

In our wonder-full, perilous journey with God, we first become friends of God. Second, we are transformed such that we see things, people, events, indeed all of creation, from God's perspective. Third, we stay with this ongoing conversion, this prophetic stance, as it turns life upside down — or, more precisely, as all hell breaks loose!

PAIRED SHARING

With a trusted companion, describe a time when you felt compelled to do something large and daunting, beyond the range of what you usually do.

- Time went slowly for me when…
- Time passed quickly for me when…
- It is too late now for me to …
- It is too soon for me to …
- It is the right time for me to …

WHERE IS THE
BIBLE IN ALL THIS?

*The truth of scripture is not about literal words,
things and concepts. The truth of scripture is about
relationships — relationships between God and us
and between us as persons.*

Jean Zaru of Ramallah

WRESTLING WITH LOVE,
MONEY and SCRIPTURE

SOME WOMEN I KNOW ARE repelled by parts of the Bible.
They object to images of God as Lord, King and Judge,
saying they find them too archaic and too patriarchal. Others
rejoice in biblical images of God as Creator, Christ and Holy
Spirit, saying they are attracted to scripture because they find
assurance and affirmation in its pages. Both groups are perplexed
by the views of the other, which can lead to judgmental ideas and
critical feelings toward those who see scripture differently. Your
interest in the Bible may be salted with wariness; I know mine is.

It is natural to wonder what dusty old words have to do with
fresh new choices. What could the Bible possibly have to say about
today's challenges with love and money?

A MIXED BIBLICAL BAG

The Bible is familiar.
Life is strange.
We bring the two together
To shed light on life.

-Avivah Gottlieb Zornberg

Some aspects of The Holy Bible are confusing and some are clarifying. Some parts are timely, addressing specific conditions at certain times of history. Others are timeless living words that carry meaning across eons. Poetic Psalms and passionate parables form a double rainbow in my mind's eye, lighting human concerns with holy radiance and prismatic color. The beauty stretches from age to age, illuminating mundane affairs with sacred wonder. Praying the Psalms can lead to awesome encounters with the Divine Author behind the text.

May Sabbath Economics and scripture shine with double radiance for you, whether you are at the cautious end of the scriptural spectrum or the carefree end of the rainbow. As poet Galway Kinnell muses: *Could it be that I am the pot of gold?*

START WITH LOVE

You shall love the Lord your God with all your heart,
and with all your soul, and with all your strength,
and with all your mind; and your neighbor as yourself.
Luke 10:27

Love offers a starting place for biblically cautious people to engage with scriptural enthusiasts. Sabbath Economics provides common ground for people of all biblical opinions. You, the person holding this, I imagine you've had some encounters with love and a variety of experiences with money. You may have direct experience with the Holy and you may be hungry for more. Stay tuned — Sabbath practices suggested in upcoming chapters may intrigue and entice you.

You and I come equipped with unique expressions of body and soul, heart and mind, will and strength. As humans imbued with individual strengths and limits, we naturally tend to develop more fully in some aspects and give less attention to others. For instance, she may tend to focus on feelings more than theories while he may trust ideas more than sensations. Love asks us to respect and nurture ALL capacities, yours and mine, ours and theirs.

"Gospel" means "*good news.*" Sabbath Economics links the good news of Jesus great invitation to lure us toward wholeness. When spiritual and material matters unite, it seems more OK to bring money matters to prayer. Love for self, God, and neighbor can ease itchy issues like debt, surplus, and neighboring. For those with eyes to see and ears to hear, scripture can nourish emotions and open you to deeper stirrings.

Bible passages can be as dense as six-grain bread, laden with meaning beyond the content, seeded with divine possibilities. Psalms and parables are especially invitational and even transformational for 21st Century folks. The ancient poems of The Psalter reflect the rawness of life as it was centuries ago and is today. People in many moods and different conditions addressed God in poetic prayers of thanks, praise, pain and lament. The Psalms are salted with feelings and seeded with sensations that nourish body and soul.

Parables offer food for the mind. Stories and similes told by Jesus 2,000 years ago were so memorable that disciples remembered and recorded them long after the end of their Teacher's life on Earth. Short punchy parables stretch human concepts, stir the imagination, confound what we think we know, and expand our minds to grapple with layers of spiritual and social meaning.

Pairing parables with Sabbath Economics directs us toward spiritual and fiscal maturity. As you and I honestly face our issues with accumulating, spending and debt, we grow up emotionally and financially. We become more aware, more able to use our personal and monetary resources in service to neighbors and Earth. Sabbath Economics offers powerful tools for the evolution of the human species and the transformation of the cosmos.

THE GOSPEL OF JOHN

In John's Gospel, we find a love beyond all labels, said Angela Khabeb. I relate to John's Gospel because I too came to the well at noon with a nameless sister from Samaria and drank Living Water. Under cover of night, I ventured up a tree with Nicodemus to climb closer to the radical rabbi named Jesus. Clenching my jaw with righteous judgment and holding my fistful of stones, I nearly cast them at the woman taken in adultery, until the generous grace of Jesus stopped me. When Lazarus died, I wept alongside Mary and Martha, and later rejoiced with the two sisters when Jesus resurrected their brother.

Jesus shook up the status quo by challenging societal expectations all the way through John's Gospel, He healed on the Sabbath, spoke to Gentile women, touched lepers, dealt with pagans and ate with sinners. Jesus spoke hard truths to men in power and caused so much political upheaval that he was given the death penalty. Even as he stared down death — not just any death, but the brutality of crucifixion — Jesus used his final hours to teach the way of love.

If I had less than a day to live, I wonder what would most concern me. For Jesus, the way was clear. His timeless words feel to me like a Great Invitation: *I give you a new commandment, that you love one another. Just as I have loved you, you also should love one another. By this everyone will know that you are my disciples, if you have love for one another.* (John 13:34-35). Jesus continued to deepen his relationship with the disciples up until shortly before he died. *I do not call you servants any longer,* he assures them, *but I have called you friends.* (John 15:15)

WHAT WOULD
JESUS WRITE?

*To read the Gospel of Matthew or Luke is to be dazzled
by one miracle after another. Thomas's Jesus never
performs a miracle and never claims that he will have
to die for the sins of humankind.*

— Erik Reece

D O YOU REMEMBER THE DAYS when WWJD bracelets
appeared on the wrists of young people across the country?
The Sabbath Economics movement does not have bracelets, but
we do find it useful to ask *What Would Jesus Do?* as we choose how
to spend our treasure, our talent and our time. Joe Dominguez
called this *creative frugality*. I think of it as *Sabbath selectivity*. Both
practices involve cutting out non-essential stuff and dedicating
ourselves to creatively — and selectively — doing what we can to
move toward greater freedom and wholeness with love and money.

THE GOSPEL OF THOMAS JEFFERSON

Perhaps something similar was on Thomas Jefferson's mind back
in 1815 when he took a pair of scissors to the King James Bible.
Jefferson cut out what he considered non-essential parts of the
four Gospels and pasted together what was left. He called it *The
Philosophy of Jesus.*

What did he cut out?
The infancy narratives. The miracles. The resurrection.

What did he keep?
The teachings.

As far as Thomas Jefferson was concerned, Jesus' life combined actions like walking, eating with followers and outcasts, going apart to pray, preaching, fishing a little, and telling stories that few seemed to understand. I can't help noticing that Jesus of Nazareth acted pretty much the same as the countless men and women who now live on the streets of this country.

To Jefferson, what mattered most was paying attention to what Jesus taught — mostly through parables — to *those with ears to hear*. By cutting out much of the version of Christianity that was being taught in American churches in the 1800s, Jefferson gave full attention to an ordinary rabbi who taught an extraordinary message of love and simplicity.

In reading Thomas Jefferson's gospel two hundred years later, it is hard not to feel disturbed — as did the Rich Young Ruler — about how difficult it is to actually follow Jesus' program. In reading Matthew and Luke, it is easy to be dazzled by the miracles overshadowing his hard teachings. Doubtless, many of us, if reading The Jefferson Bible* *(retitled by Beacon Press for later publication), today would find it simply too hard to bear Jesus' relentless demands, imploring us to become much better people — inside and out.

Jefferson's gospel offers simple clarifications of Jesus' teachings. The list isn't long:

- Love God, self and neighbor with all your heart, mind, soul and strength.

- Treat people the way we want to be treated.
- Do not judge others.
- Do not bear grudges.
- Return violence with compassion.
- Pray in secret; don't boast about righteousness.
- Work for peaceful resolutions and justice for all.
- Don't be a hypocrite.
- Be modest and unpretentious.
- The Sabbath is for us; honor it.

THE GOSPEL OF DIDYMOS JUDAS THOMAS

Thomas is the Aramaic word for *twin*. Eons before Thomas Jefferson cut and pasted his version of Jesus' teachings, another Thomas wrote a similar gospel in Coptic, an Egyptian variant of the Greek language. It was hidden in a cave for centuries, and discovered in 1945. The Gospel of Thomas focuses entirely on the teachings of Jesus, wise and witty sayings through which you and I may discover nuggets of spiritual guidance as we compose our own money-love story.

The Gospel of Thomas begins with this Prologue: *These are the secret sayings that the living Jesus spoke, and Didymos Judas Thomas recorded.* Three examples:

- In Thomas 3:4–5, Jesus said, "*When you know yourselves, then you will be known, and you will understand that you are children of the living Father. But if you do not know yourselves, then you live in poverty, and you are the poverty.*"
- In Thomas 5:1–2, Jesus said, "*Know what is in front of*

your face, and what is hidden from you will be disclosed to you. For there is nothing hidden that will not be revealed."
- In Thomas 70:1–2, Jesus said, *"If you bring forth that which is within you, what you have will save you. If you do not have that within you, what you do not have within will kill you."*

A MONK NAMED THOMAS

The rush and pressure of modern life are a form, perhaps the most common form, of its innate violence. To allow oneself to be carried away by a multitude of conflicting concerns, to surrender to too many demands, to commit oneself to too many projects, to want to help everyone in everything, is to succumb to social violence.

Thomas Merton

- When the bills keep piling up, and I have to work harder to keep from going deeper into debt, how can I afford to rest?
- When I get exhausted and wonder how I got here, where can I turn for help?
- When I tell others, "I am so busy," do I feel these words as a badge of pride, or a true lament that I am stretched so thin?
- How can I take a real break from work while immersed in a culture of busy-ness that measures my worth by what I accomplish?
- When my calendar is booked solid, how do I find time for Sabbath rest?

- What would it be like to take a day off work and go fishing?
- If I sat in the sun, or watched a movie, would I be any less worthy?
- What would it be like if I spent my energy only on myself today?
- Would I lose all my friends and connections if I took a break from social media today?

CONTEMPLATIVE WRITING

No two people take away the same thing from any piece of writing. Each writer offers different insights. Perhaps you and I will never be on the same page as Didymos Judas Thomas or Thomas Jefferson or Thomas Merton. Perhaps the best we can hope is to simply get to know ourselves a little better through contemplative writing.

Something More happens when we sit before a blank page or a blank screen to ponder not only what is before our face but — even more essentially — what is hidden in our soul.

Contemplative writing is a time-tested way to bring forth *that which is within you.*

Contemplative writing can reliably reveal *that which is hidden, that which will save you.*

- How might Love be calling me into right relationship with money?
- What does this year's tax return tell me?
- What does next year's checkbook ask me to consider?
- Which sources within my faith tradition can best guide my choices about saving?

- Which gospel texts encourage me to share with the needy?
- Who can guide me in *creative frugality* as I choose to cut my discretionary spending?
- What choices am I called to make in how and where to invest my surplus?
- How might my surplus money foster freedom for others?
- Where might I invest time and tenderness on behalf of people in economic bondage?
- How might my congregation become better attuned to investing our common surplus?
- In the past week, when and how did I behave as a good steward?
- How might I celebrate this free flow?
- When was I least generous? With whom?
- How might I mend these missed opportunities?
- How much stewardship is enough?

WRITING YOUR OWN APHORISMS

If you have money, don't lend it at interest. Rather, give it to someone from whom you won't get it back.
Jesus in Gospel of Thomas 95

The aphorism is the oldest written art form on the planet, practiced by Chinese scholars, Greek philosophers, Old Testament authors, Jesus, Buddha and Mohammed. Aphorisms are the literary loners we find in sources including Ecclesiastes, Proverbs, the I Ching, the Gospel of Thomas and the Upanishads.

An aphorism is a turn of phrase that achieves maximum impact by making a sudden reversal. Aphorisms make verbal pirouettes and teach the mind to do the twist. Aphorisms are as sprightly as ever in our sound-bite era, because we need incisive sayings to help us see life more smartly in dark times and in light.

Begin by browsing through these terse statements.

Now it is your turn to try your hand at composing an aphorism Choose one and use it as model for your own.

Enjoy the challenge of combining imagery, brevity, wit and paradox.

- Buddha: *Be lamps unto yourselves.*
- Confucius: *What you do not want done to yourself, do not do to others.*
- Heraclitus: *One cannot step into the same river twice, for the water in which you first stepped has flowed on.*
- Mohammed: *An hour's contemplation is better than a year's adoration.*
- Epicurus: *A man is wealthy in proportion to the things he can do without.*
- Seneca: *Whatever can happen at any time can happen today.*
- François-René de Chateaubriand: *Love decreases when it ceases to increase.*
- William Blake: *Energy is eternal delight.*
- Ben Franklin: *A good example is the best sermon.*
- Ralph Waldo Emerson: *God builds temples in the heart on the ruins of churches and religions.*
- Henry David Thoreau: *Be a Columbus to whole new worlds within you, opening new channels, not of trade, but of thought.*
- Mark Twain: *The lack of money is the root of all evil.*
- Barbara Kruger: *I shop, therefore I am.*
- Pete Nelson: *Wondering is more stimulating than certainty.*

CHOOSING WHAT MATTERS MOST

Creative frugality is a double win — for our wallets and for our world.

- Joe Dominguez

J OE DOMINGUEZ WAS DEDICATED TO creative frugality. He was a successful financial analyst on Wall Street before retiring at the of thirty-one. Joe and Vicki Robin co-founded The New Road Map Foundation in Seattle, an all-volunteer, nonprofit organization that promotes a humane, sustainable future for our world. They gave me practical ways to step off the consumer treadmill of more-is-better. They gave me tools to stop blaming *the powers that be* and showed me how to take responsibility for my own financial choices. They helped me face the truth that the major driving force behind our planetary plight is not the military-industrial complex or the federal budget or defense spending. You and I feel powerless to change the big stuff. Their teachings showed me that the real problem is our (my) patterns of consumer spending here in North America. It is empowering to know that my (our) relentless demand for more-more-more is the major driving force behind oceans clogged with plastic waste, polluted air and soil depleted by chemicals. Such knowledge is a source of great power. Choosing what matters most in consumer spending is something I (we) *can* do something about.

I chose to follow Joe Dominguez and Vicki Robin's steps to

financial independence, and it turned my life around. A few friends and I followed their early guidelines, printed on mimeographed work sheets that preceded publication of their book in 1992. *Your Money or Your Life: Transforming Your Relationship with Money and Achieving Financial Independence* is a trustworthy text. I highly recommend the revised fourth edition.

If you do choose the way of creative frugality, it will empower you to make maximum contribution to the world, while also fulfilling your own happiness and wholeness along the way.

Choices abound.

What do you choose to have and to hold?
What do you choose to spend and to give?

Whose words do you choose to ignore?
Whose guidance do you choose to heed?

A PERSONAL TESTIMONY

I have learned that the most reliable source of spiritual guidance is beyond belief. True inner guidance waits on the other side of certainty, out in the realm of *not-knowing*. It is a paradox. I continue to wrestle with the meaning of this.

Paradox comes from two Greek words. *Para* means beyond and *dox* means belief. For me, *beyond belief* means more than *unbelievable*. In my experience, paradox means *beyond my current understanding. And, wildly enough, Para translates as Money on Google Translator*

What happened at my father's deathbed was beyond understanding. The mystery of it left me to dwell for a very long time in the realm of *not-knowing* until, eventually, I received guidance about next steps with love and money.

It is not easy or comfortable to be stuck in a state of *not-knowing*. Distractions abound. It takes patience and courage to stay with it, to listen beneath the surface of things. Paradox insists upon trust. Without setting our intention to trust something we do not yet understand, we cannot be baptized into The Deep

It takes time — often a long, long time — for deeper truths to reach our conscious awareness, and even longer to take right action. The discipline of choosing what matters most in matters of love and money requires us to commit to the Sabbath Economics journey for the long haul. Living with paradox beyond belief requires that we not depend upon outmoded habits or invest in quick reactions. Instead, finding guidance beyond belief invites us to immerse ourselves in the Ocean of Light and wait for truth to show itself to our Inner Guide.

SABBATH PRACTICE IN NOT-KNOWING

- Sit or lie flat in a secure place where you feel safe.
- Focus attention of the Breath of Life.
- Let each breath fill you with nourishment.
- Let each breath go with gratitude.
- Exhale even more fully and let go of memories about what lies behind you.
- Inhale even more deeply and let go of ideas about what lies ahead of you.
- Follow the light that is near you.
- Renew your intention to trust this mysterious spark of light.
- Exhale any anxiety or worry.

- Inhale thanks for this spark of light.
- Breathe slowly into the realm of not-knowing.
- Engage your active imagination.
- Imagine yourself as an inlet near the ocean, an open and receptive inlet.
- Let yourself receive any currents of awareness that float your way.
- Let yourself accept any insights that flow into you from any direction.
- Breathe in all currents of cognition, emotion or sensation.
- Breathe out all currents of sensation, cognition or emotion.
- Rest in receptivity, a simple inlet at the edge of the Ocean of Light.
- When you rise, leave your old beliefs in the light.
- Go about your day with renewed intention to expand your capacity for paradox.

KNOWING
YOUR FLOW

Money travels everywhere. It crosses all boundaries,
language and cultures.
Money, like water, ripples at some level through every
life and place.
It can carry our love or our fear.
It can flood some of us such that we drown in a toxic
sense of power over others.
It can nourish and water the principles of freedom,
community and sharing.
Money can affirm life, or it can be used to demean,
diminish, or destroy life.
It is neither evil nor good: money is an instrument.
We invented it, and it belongs squarely in the human
experience.
Money can be used by and merged with the longings
and passions of our soul.

- Lynne Twist

GOOD STORIES LEAVE US WONDERING what's coming next. Great stories always surprise us. My money-love stories and yours are not just about analyzing data and stating conclusions. Good money-love stories keep raising questions. Hidden stories, especially those that emerge from puzzling questions, keep bringing us back into the flow of tangible, embodied emotions.

They keep leading us toward surprising discoveries, and giving us unexpected tastes of grace.

Curious questions invite us to walk new paths of exploration and discovery into stories we cannot yet hear. Queries can be like river currents: barely visible from shore, we have to get into the river before we see how questions flow into actions, and how contemplatively immersing ourselves in Love's Spirit can surprise us with unanticipated forms of unfolding.

When your money-love stories and mine join into the powerful flow of Mystery as it pulls souls toward wholeness, these stories help us notice and name the currents of divine purpose moving through our bloodstream. They shine sunlight on the flow of Living Water that comes to buoy us up during hard times, and carry us toward healthier choices and more lifegiving decisions. Honest, vulnerable stories — shared with generosity and listened to with tenderness — can go a long way toward clearing the stagnant pools in our soul that have been muddied by shame, blame, pain, guilt or judgment. Writing, reading and hearing true money-love stories can reduce human isolation, build community and restore creation.

Truthful money-love stories can also remind us to enjoy and express gratitude. I have told many grateful stories of interacting with the Haitian people in letters, articles, books, sermons and presentations since those times when countless community leaders, market-women and peasant-men welcomed us into their homes, churches and circles of support. Among the Haitian people, I heard songs of praise and felt the power of collective action as, astonishingly, the poorest people in this hemisphere met extreme poverty by giving thanks to God.

In these pages, you've read many stories of money and love, including portions of my own small story. I include mine because writing is a time-tested way of letting go into the larger story. Personal stories have a surprising power to enfold us into the

Great Love that transcends all our stories, and seeks to coax our shyness into words.

JUDITH'S TRANSFORMATIVE STORY

This word is a hidden word. It comes in the darkness of night. To enter this darkness, put away all voices and sounds, all images and likenesses. For no image has reached into the soul's foundation where God herself, with her own being, is effective.

Meister Eckhart, 1260–1328

About the time I learned to sing *Jesus loves me, this I know,* Grandma took me to the narthex of Acreage Community Church and lifted me up so I could touch my own name inscribed on the Cradle Roll. "You are a baptized child," she assured me. "Baptism means that Christ will always look after you and Jesus is your friend for life. Always remember this."

Did I remember Grandma's counsel? Yes, for a while. I remembered that Jesus was my friend during Dad's alcoholic rages, when I climbed into the safety of my top bunk, covered my head with a blanket and asked Jesus to protect Mom, me and my little brothers. And Jesus did protect us, every time. Dad stormed and swore, but never hit anyone. After each crisis passed, my prayer would become less fervent and more automatic, repeating the lines of *Now I lay me down to sleep,* the bedtime prayer I learned from my mother.

As I got busier with studies, babysitting my brothers and working at the public library after school and also on Saturdays, Jesus faded into the background. By 1957, when I started college, Jesus was nowhere to be found. Chapel attendance, however, was required by Pacific University. It had been founded as a college for girls by Tabitha Brown, a Congregational missionary. A Congregational Board of Directors then set policies of compulsory chapel. Students had no choice. I sat through weekly chapel services, but my mind was not on Jesus. Romance trumped religion. Personal dramas of first love and engagement occupied my attention, not Jesus. David and I married in 1959 and transferred to Washington State University, where chapel attendance was not compulsory. I soon concluded that nothing life-giving was to be found in church.

About the time The Beatles recorded *Abbey Road,* I took a new road to Shasta Abbey. Burdened with wifely and motherly responsibilities, my shy soul-seed was buried so deep that I barely knew I had one. I sensed there must be more to life than household duties and carpools, but had no idea what that was or how to find it. A Catholic-Buddhist-Marxist friend offered to teach me to meditate, so I took him up on it. While the kids were in school, we sat side by side on cushions facing a blank wall and silently counted each breath to ten, then started over. Jim did, anyway. I could never get past three before my mind went scampering off. Still, I sensed some benefit in meditation and wanted more.

Jim recommended Tassajara Zen Center near Big Sur. There I could study under his Zen teacher, but I was tired of dominant males telling me what to do. Sensing new freedom in the voices of the rising women's liberation movement, I chose a female abbot to introduce me to the art and practice of Buddhist meditation. I was excited at the chance to go on retreat to Shasta Abbey and asked Teri and Roy — who lived in a teepee off the grid — to care for my children. My hippie friends brought guitars, sang with the kids and baked cookies in exchange for hot showers and a warm waterbed.

Roshi Jiyu Kennett was a somber, sturdy woman from England who had studied meditation in Japan. Robed in brown, she led the monks and me single file into the *zendo* where we sat cross-legged on hard, round cushions called *zafus*. The opening ceremony involved gongs, gestures, incense and chants. The most challenging part about chanting in unison for me was the names of bodhisattvas going all the way back to the beginning of Roshi Kennett's Buddhist lineage. All of them were guys. I had no clue to their stories, or why we should revere them. Stumbling over the unfamiliar Asian syllables and intonations, I tried to act cool while the real monks rhythmically chanted long sequences of names and wafted incense around the *zendo*.

I was relieved when the ritual was over and we could finally settle into silence. Even so, I was far too scattered to focus on more than three breaths in a row. The goal was to quiet the mind and count breaths to ten, but I never made it. I managed brief moments of stillness until my thoughts careened off the path and dumped me into thorny thickets of troubled emotions.

My legs ached after a few hours, and my butt throbbed. I was praying for a stretch-break and a walk in the woods, but lunch was served in the *zendo*, seated on our *zafus*. One kitchen monk handed each meditator a bowl. Two more monks walked slowly around the circle; one carried a two-handled pot and the other ladled veggie-rice soup into each bowl. No spoons. I did my best to sip without spilling. After the meal, the first monk returned with a kettle of hot water and poured a bit into each bowl. I watched and learned that this is how monks wash the dishes. Swish hot water around to cleanse your bowl, drink the water, and the job is done.

I was tired and sore during the afternoon meditation session, far too bothered by physical discomfort to nod off. Through tall windows, long beams of September sunlight spilled across the hardwood floor. As I watched them move toward me, I felt the first glimmers of peace. Before I could register the gift of a momentarily quiet mind, Light and Love flooded my entire *bodymindheartsoul*. This was not ordinary sunlight, but a profound embrace of such great warmth and power that it took my breath away. Suffused with light and completely confused, I heard a firm, warm voice say, *These are not your saints. Come unto me.*

I could not comprehend what was happening.

Trembling before the Sacred Presence, I was completely engulfed in wonder. Stunned and awed, I remember being grateful that I was already sitting on the floor, for surely I would have fallen to the ground, as Moses did before the burning bush.

These are not your saints. That must mean the bodhisattvas whose names we just finished chanting (Well, it was the Buddhist monks who had chanted. I had just mumbled along.)

True, these bodhisattvas are unknown to me.
They are certainly not my saints.
But who are my saints?
I could not remember the name of a single Christian saint.

Come unto me.
Those are words Jesus spoke to the disciples.
Or maybe to the crowd.
Did he say, Come unto me, all who are troubled?
Or Come unto me, all who bear heavy burdens."
What were the exact words? Can't remember.
Which gospel are they in? No idea.

At least I know who The Light of the World is.
But why would Jesus address me, on a hard cushion
in a Buddhist zendo?

A shy soul, pretending to chant names of the
bodhisattvas?
An ordinary mom, doing my best to meditate?

The Voice didn't sound human.
Sort of like Charleston Heston playing God in a movie.
The Voice was unbelievably loving.
Totally accepting.
Warmly inviting.
Filled with goodness and mercy.
Beckoning me to come unto Christ.

I sat stunned and shaking, with no clue what was going on. My whole *bodymindheartsoul* was vibrant, alive with greater joy and peace than I had ever imagined possible. Entranced by Loving Light, my thoughts kept bouncing around…

What just happened?

I tried to reason it out. *"These are not your saints"* must mean that I am not meant to follow the Buddhist lineage of Roshi Jiyu Kennett. The last words — *Come unto me* — carried even greater intensity and aliveness. What could all this possibly mean?

I remained at the monastery as planned, but spent my days puzzling over my mysterious encounter with Jesus. I did not dare tell Roshi Kennett about any of this, partly because I had no way to explain the unexplainable, and partly because I feared being judged for letting Christ into a community dedicated to Buddhist teachings and practice.

I drove home in a daze, moving automatically down Interstate

5 from Mount Shasta to Chico. I greeted my sons and daughter, heard everyone's stories of the fun they'd had together, and hugged Roy and Teri goodbye.

My husband was off, God knows where. There was no grownup at home to confide in, even if I had been able to find words for the experience. It had been so odd, so compelling and so powerful that I knew it would sound crazy. Later I did attempt to explain to my husband what had happened, but he was so scornful — and did label me crazy — that I realized I'd made a big mistake by telling him. I felt like I had tossed my pearls before swine.

I might have sought pastoral counseling, if I'd had a pastor, but I was unchurched. Sermons bored me and I'd been skeptical about the Bible since adolescence. Barely thirty at the time, I had no idea how central the Sabbath is for most Christians and Jews, nor did I understand that God's grace had guided me into a profound sort of Sabbath — among silent monks in the *zendo*.

Something still kept eating at me though. Something made me restless and left me feeling incomplete, but had I no idea what was missing. Well, I did have some idea. Marital intimacy was missing, as well as a sense of trust in the man I had promised to love and obey 'til death do us part. But there was something more, something just out of sight, far beyond the scope of my horizon. The search for this elusive something — this mysterious pearl of great price — was what had led me to a Zen monastery in the first place. Why had I been embraced and addressed by the Living Christ in the company of Buddhist strangers?

> *What was I meant to do with all this?*
> *Better just forget it.*
> *But I couldn't forget it.*

*I had been found and touched by a Love that would
not let me go.*

In the contemplative practice of Sabbath Economics, we allow
our psychological boundaries to go fluid. We step off the shore
and enter deep waters. Fluidity can be scary because we never
know what we may find. Or become. Yet, when we do surrender
to the deep waters of Mystery, we know we will never be the same
when we come back to shore.

KNOW YOUR BREATH FLOW: A SABBATH PRACTICE

*I would love to live like a river flows, carried by the
surprise of its own unfolding.*

John O'Donohue

Breath is the most primal and natural flow. You and I can choose
to take a Sabbath pause at a moment's notice by consciously
attending to our breath. Here's how:

- Sit in a comfortably supported posture, or lie down
  on your back.
- Breathe just the way you normally do.
- Notice where the breath comes and goes most easily,
  in which part of the body.
- Does breath flow most naturally through nostrils?
- Does breath flow most readily down your throat?
- Does it most naturally and easily fill your chest?
- Or is it easiest to notice your breath-flow by sensing
  the rise and fall of your belly?

- Rest attention wherever you find the greatest ease in your breath-flow.
- Gently notice your breath flow in and out from that part of your body.
- If attention strays off into memories or plans, exhale fully.
- Let go of any distractions and return your focus to the place of most ease.
- Breathe there until you feel ready to stop the practice.
- Thank the part of your body that so readily receives and gives breath-flow.
- You may want to tell it you will return soon to enjoy its natural flow.

EXAMINING YOUR MONEY FLOW

One way to know your flow is through a spiritual practice more commonly known these days as *examination of consciousness, or conscientiousness*. Roman Catholic monks, nuns and priests consider it a basic form of daily prayer, and call it by its Latin name, *examen (pronounced ex-a-men)*. If you're curious and want to give it a try, this is your invitation to experiment with an ancient spiritual practice.

1. Saint Ignatius practiced and taught this five-step process:
2. Become aware of God's presence.
3. Review the day with gratitude.
4. Pay attention to your emotions.
5. Choose one feature of the day and pray from it.
6. Look toward tomorrow

Begin by shaking off any judgments, good or bad. *Examen* is not about meeting anyone's external criteria or pleasing some distant judge. Seeing your true flow of money is simply one form of personal fact-finding. The reflective *examen* practice is an opportunity to re-examine the flow of money through your life, and to notice how you manage and direct it, or neglect it. The *examen* offers greater self-knowledge so that you may make a more conscious choice to align earning, giving and spending with your highest vision of yourself, your values and your commitments. When done on a regular basis, the *examen* practice may also give you a peek at how well your flow fits, not only with who you are today, but also with who you are becoming.

I invite you to pause as you turn attention from others' stories and focus on your own. When you have a free hour, make a cup of tea, sit in a comfortable place, open your journal and pick up a pen. Give yourself a chance to bring more consciousness into your relationship with love and money. The ways we earn or acquire money can suppress us — or free us. Acquisition matters. The ways we spend money have an effect on others. How we give money makes a difference in the world. The *examen* is your chance to true the course of money flowing through your life. It is an important practice, courageous and empowering.

- How much, or how little, are you aware of the flow of money in your life?
- Are you ready to see it in black and white?
- Are you mindful of how money comes to you?
- Does it come through unhealthy forms of work?
- Does money come to you through relationships that deplete or exploit you?

- Are you consciously allocating where you want your money to go?

When you see the way money flows through your hands, it will give you power to choose.

- What do you notice when you look at your bank statement?
- Which desires and responsibilities do you see in your check register?
- What priorities and patterns do you see in your credit-card receipts?
- What's missing?

BENEDICTION:
A HYMN FROM the VEDIC TRADITION
by Yogi Philip Goldberg

As different streams
have their sources in different places,
and all mingle their water in the sea,
so, O Lord, the different paths which we take
through different tendencies,
various though they appear,
crooked or straight,
all will lead to Thee.

GIVING YOUR BEST

You must do the thing you think you cannot do.
Eleanor Roosevelt

GRANDMA'S JAPANESE GRANDDAUGHER

CORDELIA DAVIS WRIGHT, MY GRANDMOTHER, suffered economic hardships during the Great Depression, yet still found it in her heart to give money to Japanese girls orphaned in World War Two. When a hit-and-run driver killed my grandfather in 1945, he left her nearly penniless. She had a home, but no pension or Social Security benefits to pay the mortgage. Grandma found work as a cook at my elementary school, and supplemented her meager wages by moving into the principal's home to care for his children when he traveled.

I remember feeling a surge of jealousy the day she showed me a deckle-edged snapshot of a Japanese girl and said, "Meet Misaki, my new granddaughter."

"But, Grandma," I protested, "I'M your granddaughter. Your only one!" An outraged eight-year-old, I turned away from a girl wearing a kimono, black hair wound up on top of her head, holding herself very straight as she stood in front of a cherry tree in blossom.

"Yes, Judy," Grandma assured me, "you are my first granddaughter, and my favorite." She pretended to wipe the pout from my face and rested a warm hand on my head. "But now you're not my only granddaughter. You have food and toys, and parents to look after you, but Misaki does not. Hers were killed in the war. She is all alone now, so I will be her grandmother as long as I can."

I loved hearing what had sparked her to send monthly donations to Christian Children's Foundation, no matter how often she repeated the story. It began with LIFE Magazine, where she saw the photo of a dirty-faced Japanese child clutching an empty bowl to her chest. The hollow-eyed urchin had been orphaned by American bombs, and this troubled my grandmother's soul. *What have we done to these little ones?* She placed the photo on her dresser, and gazed into the haunted little eyes before sleep. *God have mercy,* she prayed.

Deep in the night, she said she felt fingers pinching the skin of her forearm, and awoke with a start. She heard a coughing sound that caused her own throat to narrow. She was working to make sense of these sensations when she heard *Turn, turn, turn* and recognized lines from an old song. Grandma did turn onto one side then, and soon felt someone nestling against her heart, filling the space her husband Leo once held was small body, bony and shivering. Oh, she realized, it's a child. It felt so natural to hold a small girl again, as she once held Margo to her heart, and Virginia ten years later.

All week she thought about this odd encounter. Turning to God, she asked, *Why have you sent me a Japanese daughter?* Grandma kept her heart turned toward Jesus, and kept asking, *What are you showing me, Lord?* No answer, at least not one she could hear.

Verna cooked beside her in the kitchen at Rigler Elementary, so Grandma asked her friend to listen. She needed help to sort things out. She described being pinched in the night. How good it felt to nestle a cold child to her heart. How she kept asking God what she was supposed to do. How she heard no clear instructions.

Verna bounced excitedly on the balls of her feet. "At church," she said," pastor told about authorities building a Japanese refugee camp near the river downtown. Do you think your dream means we need to go there and cook for the war orphans?"

"But," Grandma protested, "I know nothing about steaming rice or seasoning fish soup. What do you know?"

"Nothing whatsoever," said Verna.

"Heavens, I have no idea how to cook in a wok." "That's right. We cook what American kids like to eat, just as Japanese women know what to cook for their kids," said Grandma, "so that probably isn't it."

"Right," mused Verna. "The girl who came in the night belongs in Japan, not Portland."

"That's it!" said Grandma. "I bet God wants me to help her, right where she is!"

"But how in the world can you do that?"

"Maybe I'll ask Reverend Hampton."

So, this is how prayer and paired sharing led my grandmother to Sabbath Economics, a path she followed for the last two decades of her life. Christian Children's Fund sent information about Misaki, who attended school in an orphanage. Every month, without fail, Grandma sent an international money order to Tokyo to cover her granddaughter's school uniforms and books.

Cordelia Davis Wright had none of the privileges that I later enjoyed in adulthood. She wouldn't have known the difference between yoga and yogurt, and in fact never experienced either, but she did know how to be generous and self-giving. Each time I visited, she proudly showed the most recent pale-blue airmail letter, and after each Japanese granddaughter graduated from high school, she showed me the photos and read notes of thanks. Grandma's sacrificial giving planted a seed in my heart. Her dedication to a succession of orphaned girls lasted all her life, and influenced the whole family. After she died, my uncle supported the next generation of Japanese schoolgirls, and his widow Charlotte continued the tradition after Dean died.

MY HAITIAN SONS

Some years after Grandma died, I contacted the international Christian Children's Fund in Haiti and was matched with Julbert Fonbrun, "a *little boy who was forsaken by his father longtime ago and lived with his mother in a poor community in northeastern Port-au-Prince called Lakou Fonten.*" I sent monthly funds for health, nutrition and education. We exchanged letters for years, and I was able to meet Julbert's family when he was ten years old. We had a cheerful, though awkward, visit in their home, a one-room house with walls of mud, a sheet iron roof and no electricity or potable water. Later, I paid school fees for his brother Estin, *a boy with good aptitude toward reading and writing.* I also funded bicycles so both could find work as delivery boys.

Sadly, I lacked sufficient financial and emotional resources to support Julbert's request to move to California and live with me. By this time, he had learned passable English. An excerpt from his letter: *You know at eighteen, I am young, but I want to tell you my dream. I have in mind to enter in a university where you live. All around your letter your words comfort me. You give me strength. Firstly, I want to be near God. Secondly, I want to be near you. I would like to follow some long studies in theology and in computers. I particularly practice soccer ball but sometimes I play basketball. The skill I would like to develop is the music because I would like to be a musician. I right now have in mind to come to California. I hope I will learn more there.*

I still regret being unable to support Julbert's college education, but his request was *beyond my light and strength,* as Quakers say.

LYNNE'S STORY

Author Lynne Twist is founder and president of the Soul of Money Institute. Her story illustrates ways of using money to express our deepest core values. As a fundraiser, she traveled all over the world and saw fear of scarcity expressed in every culture and by people in every economic condition. "Whether we live in resource-poor circumstances or resource-rich ones, even if we're loaded with more money and goods than we could possibly dream of wanting or needing, most of us live with scarcity as an underlying assumption. But scarcity," she concludes, "is an unexamined and false system of assumptions, opinions and beliefs from which most people view the world as a place where we are in constant danger of not having our needs met. In scarcity, any drop in the balance sheet becomes a loss that diminishes our sense of self-worth. But scarcity is a lie," she concludes. "Sufficiency is the truth."

The underlying principle of sufficiency is flow. "Treat money like water," she says. It should flow through our lives, not accumulate and stagnate. When we are rooted in sufficiency, the back-and-forth movement of money and love feels natural. The flow feels healthy and true. When we can allow money and love to flow freely, we feel good about that. When we can stay grounded in the Inward Light, we can use money's power to do good. We feel fulfillment and joy when we direct the flow toward our highest ideals and commitments.

"When I made that first contribution to The Hunger Project it realigned my priorities. My financial life started to be more in alignment with my deep sense of self and soul. I began to have an experience of prosperity that was unrelated to any quantity of money or acquisitions. I could feel this alignment within myself, and I had done that through my use of money. That was the place where the tide turned in me. It was so surprising that money, this very thing I had used and seen others use to perpetuate accumulation, depletion, and making myself important with wine and art and stuff, ended up being the *same instrument* I eventually used to express my love for people and my affirmation of life, and to share my deepest dreams. Once that instrument, or vehicle called money, was in alignment with my soul, that was when the prosperity, joy, and sufficiency started to flourish. It wasn't in the money, but in its use as an instrument of soul.

"I learned the lesson of sufficiency from a group of women in Harlem. About seventy-five of us met in the basement of an old church to talk about The Hunger Project. I knew these women did not have much to give, and felt nervous about asking them to contribute. After I made my pitch, there was a long silence. After a bit, an older woman near the back stood up. She said 'Girl, to me money is a lot like water. For some folks it rushes through their life like a raging river. For me, money comes in a little trickle. But I want to pass it on in a way that does the most good for the most folks. I see that as my right and my responsibility. It is also my joy. I have fifty dollars in my purse that I earned from doing wash for some folks, and I want to give it to you.' Others soon followed, and I received over $500 that evening. That money was more precious to me than any I'd gotten before, because of the integrity with which it was given.

"It is a powerful, miraculous thing to use money as an expression of our deepest values. It is a practice, however, and I'm still working on it. I waste money. I buy products that are part of the problem rather than part of the solution. I get excited about money and disappointed about money and frustrated and conflicted over money issues. But I am also on a path, in a practice, that I'm sharing with you because I believe it is useful and important in our time. I'm seeing that more and more of us are awake to our higher commitments, concerned about how we're living and offering to contribute to the process taking place all around us now."

The tide turns when you and I focus attention and intention both inward, to the light within, and outward to the harsh realities suffered by "the least of these."

In the clear light of Love, we can see that *not-enoughness* is a lie. When we focus on hardships borne by the working poor, we can see the sufficiency and resiliency that dwells within. Then you and I will know one thing for sure: that we all *have* enough, and we all *are* enough, to use love and money for the common good.

PAIRED SHARING

The work of turning the tide is to sustain our integrity while life's hardships disturb our equilibrium, and to keep our balance as priorities are rearranged by the Beloved's invitation to respond. In conversation with a trusted friend, describe:

- A time when you worked *shoulder to shoulder* with others in a sustained effort to make the economic system work for "the least of these."
- Describe someone you know personally, or someone you met through reading, whose story gave you strength to do more than you thought you could.

WRITING YOUR STORY

Like musicians who wait in silence for the music to come out of the forest of their hearts, we wait on each other's stories. The purpose of story is to lead us back to what matters, and to show us how everything is connected as part of something larger.

Mark Nepo

WHEN YOU AND I REACH *out* to hug loved ones, we don't stop to think why we're doing it. We simply open our arms and embrace them. We wrap our arms around our nearest and dearest so we can hold them close to our hearts, with no advance planning. We just do it. But when you and I reach *in* to explore our hidden truths about love and money, self-embrace does not happen so easily, or so naturally. We tend to procrastinate, sometimes for decades.

So why don't you and I embrace all the parts of us, known and unknown, as we buckle down to do the work of self-reflection?

Here's how it went for me yesterday, as I tried to write this chapter. I felt restless, so I got up from the desk and went to the kitchen for a glass for water. I noticed how chilly I felt, so I decided to make tea. While waiting for the pot to boil, I spotted a cracked cup on the shelf. I carried it back to the desk and arranged a few pens in it. Then I took six new yellow pencils from the box and sharpened them. I put them in among the pens, arranged everything into a little bouquet, and stood back to admire my artistry.

I heard the kettle whistle. I walked back to the kitchen and watched the green tea steep in a black mug that declares *STRENGTH* in bold white letters. I thought fondly of Christina, who recently gave me this mug, and decided to send her an email. I carried my tea to the study, closed the cover of *Sabbath Economics: A Spiritual Guide to Linking Love with Money,* and pushed the book to the edge of the desk. I tapped the keyboard, opened Chrome and instantly became distracted by a barrage of messages. An hour later, I realized I had forgotten all about writing that thank-you note to Christina.

What is it that pulls me off track from doing the tasks I set for myself? Self-doubt is the first culprit. Doubt darkens my good intentions, especially when I'm trying to write something difficult, like my own story of love and money. When I pick up a pen or sit down at the keyboard to begin, fear can freeze the fingers.

How about you?

At this point in the process, you might blurt, *Where am I! How the heck do I know!* How am I supposed to answer the Creator's first question when I can't even concentrate on something simple like, *What am I most grateful for today? For what am I least grateful?* Doubt grows even more daunting when the reflection questions involve something extremely challenging like, *How do I see myself relating love to money these days, as I examine the way I conduct my life?*

When you and I sit shivering before the blank page — girding our loins to wade into questions that ripple surface waters atop deep reservoirs of emotion — it is natural to be afraid. Money and love relationships throb with passions and hates, hopes and hurts, disasters and dreams. Money-love relationships are also laden with beliefs that you and I keep tucked into our secret selves, covered with layers of meaning that have never seen the light of day. It can be terrifying for us to bring long-buried, hidden meanings out of the shadows and onto the page.

> To get the ball rolling, it helps to remember your intentions:
> How much do I really want financial independence?
> How much do I truly want to be free of feelings of deficiency and confusion?
> How much do I deeply desire to be at peace with love and money?

Sabbath Economics questions prompt us to reveal the essence of who we truly are. Initially, we tackle composing our story privately by writing in our journal. Later perhaps, we define and refine our truths by speaking to one friend in Paired Sharing, or to a larger community in circles of trust.

But before you dive in to the story-prompts, it helps to remember that each of us is utterly unique. You and I are created in the image and likeness of the Creator of the Universe. When we remember how unconditionally and eternally the Beloved loves us, this reality strengthens us. When you and I grow in Love until we can keep it foremost in our attention and intentions, we also grow courageous enough to face our fears, and strong enough to expose the deepest, truest parts of ourselves to the Light. As long as we can remain rooted and grounded in Love (or return to it when we stray) we are equipped to go deep beneath surface doubts and are enabled to pull up hidden meanings from the bedrock strata of our individuality.

TWENTY STORY-PROMPTS

1. Which good words best describe yourself as you are now?
2. Which good words describe the way you were as a child?
3. Which good stories illustrate the essence of you, now and as a kid?
4. How did love and money influence you during childhood?
5. What made you happiest when you were ten?
6. At age ten, what did you want to be when you grew up?
7. How did love and money influence you during adolescence?
8. At age twenty, what did you want to be when you grew up?
9. What brought you the greatest fulfillment when you were twenty?
10. What kinds of adversity did you face in your first two decades of life?
11. What held you together during hard times, then and in the following years?
12. How did your family's faith tradition or religion shape your views and values?
13. We all live with inner contradictions. How would you describe some of yours?
14. What have you done in your life that you are really proud to tell about?
15. What helps you chart a course of action and stick with it?
16. What brings you the greatest fulfillment now?

17. How is your sense of satisfaction related to money and love?
18. If you didn't have to work for a living, what would you do with your time?
19. Whose death has most transformed your life?
20. If you knew you were going to die within a year, how would you spend the year?

MICHAEL B'S STORY
WHAT CANST THOU SAY?

"A year after I was diagnosed with aggressive brain cancer, I had completed all the available medical treatments, but my prognosis wasn't good... For twenty years before my diagnosis, I'd participated in Quaker communities and had come to see the heart of Quaker practice as deeply listening for and naming how we are being both broken open and pulled toward wholeness."

What canst thou say? George Fox asked Margaret Fell. *Christ saith this, and the apostles say this; but what canst thou say?*

"Early Friends invite us to vulnerably name what is most tender and alive in our experience (so)...I decided to adapt the practice that grows from the question 'What canst thou say?' as a treatment for brain cancer. I sought out partners who could help me with... opening myself to the healing power of stories — crafting new narratives from my own inner dialogue about who I am, telling stories about my experience with others, and letting others' stories move and change me."

Interested readers will find more about Michael Bischoff's experience in *The Healing Power of Stories*, a Quaker pamphlet listed in Resources. Now in recovery from a devastating season with brain cancer, he testifies to the power of practicing *The*

Healing Power of Stories. Author Michael closes his account with five intriguing queries:

AGENCY:

What do we have control over in our relationships with love and money?

COHERENCE:

How do our varied stories fit together and make sense?

SUPPORT:

Who has been there, riding shotgun, through your journey with love and money?

COMMUNION:

Which circles of trust, support and accountability can we count on in the future?

REDEMPTION:

Which experiences with love and money — even those that resulted in trauma, suffering and loss — might contain threads of a 'silver lining'?

From the perspective of ego-selves that want to stay hidden, nothing is more terrifying than putting our truths on the page. The Essence-parts of ourselves, however, yearn to live in The Way, The Truth and The Life of Love. Like all kinds of writing, once you and I can get past initial barriers of fear and doubt, our truths will flow onto the page. Once we dare to write our real words about love and money, we will stand revealed, unconcealed and undefended, in touch at last with who we truly are. Intentional writing about love and money will change you.

Unexpected discoveries always do.

So, for now it's OK to have no idea where you stand at this moment, faced with so many questions linking love and money. It's not easy being green.

Start where you want and stop when you like.

WHY WRITE YOUR MONEY AUTOBIOGRAPHY?

Guidelines compiled by Dale Stitt for Ministry of Money

It may seem strange to you that we are suggesting you write a Money Autobiography. Why would anyone ever want to do such an exercise?

What good can come from exploring past experiences while searching for answers about our relationship with money?

We believe that unexamined experiences cause the most difficulty.

We also believe that money is a very potent ingredient in our daily lives.

We work with it, use it, play with it, fear it, and find ourselves controlled by it far more often than most of us really want to admit.

The people we know who have "found some freedom" in their relationship with money are those who spent some time thinking about it and exploring their feelings about it.

A Money Autobiography is one way to begin the process of reviewing our history and exploring our relationship with money. It is not magic. It will not solve our money problems, or answer all our questions. But this exercise can give us insights and provide us with some answers about why we do what we do, and think the way we think.

In time, this exercise may even lead to a new, healthier relationship with money.

How to Prepare for Writing Your Money Autobiography:

- Take a few minutes right now to read over the forty-eight questions below.
- Put the questions aside for a day or so, allowing them to work in your soul.
- Set aside some time to write your thoughts.
- We do not expect you to answer all of the questions, rather we invite you to share your written (3–5 pages) response to whatever you find most important to you.

YOUR HISTORY and RELATIONSHIP WITH MONEY

1. What were your childhood messages around money?
2. What was your father's attitude about money? Your mother's attitude?
3. Did your parents ever fight about money?
4. Who in your family made the money decisions?
5. Would you call your parent(s): Generous, Cautious, Stingy?
6. What sort of neighborhood(s) did you grow up in?
7. Did your family own or rent your abode(s)?
8. Do you own or rent now?
9. How would you describe your early personal experiences with money?
10. Magical? Worrisome? Fun? Scarce? Enough? Something else?

11. What happened that led to your early decisions about money?

12. Did you ever steal money or shoplift as a child? If so, did you get caught?

13. What did you learn from that experience?

14. Which statement best represents your current relationship to or with money?

15. I am just like my (mom, dad, parents, grandparent, caregiver) when it comes to dealing with money!

16. I am just the opposite of my (mom, dad, parents, grandparents, caregivers, others) when it comes to dealing with money!

17. Am I somewhere in between?

18. What leads you to your conclusion?

19. Was/is anyone in your family in a labor union?

20. What was your attitude toward the trade union movement growing up? Today?

21. Have you ever experienced unemployment or received public assistance?

22. Has anyone in your family? What was that like?

23. Have you ever gone through bankruptcy or foreclosure? How did that feel?

24. Did your parents play the stock market? What happened?

25. What messages regarding "savings" and financial security did you grow up with?

26. How have you invested, and how actively have you tried to manage your investments?

27. If you are or were in a significant relationship, how would you describe the way you and your partner made money decisions?

28. How did/does your relationship with money impact

your marriage, your sex life, your play-life, your prayer life?

29. Does this way of relating to money look anything like your parents'?

30. Do you ever worry about having enough money?

31. Do you ever worry about running out of money and becoming dependent upon others?

32. Where does the worry come from?

33. What kind of personal debt burden do you now carry?

34. Do you use consumer credit cards?

35. Carry a mortgage or personal/ business loans?

36. Have you ever had tax problems?

37. Currently the word that best describes your attitude about money is _____

38. Why? Is this attitude consistent with your deeply held values and/or religious beliefs?

39. How does the disparity between those who are wealthy and those who are poor impact you?

40. Do you ever feel guilty about the amount of money you have compared to others?

41. What do you want your relationship with money to look like?

42. What is missing for you in your current relationship with money?

43. Were there explicit or implicit moral values around issues of work, consumption and ways of handling money in your family?

44. In your church? In your school?

45. Do you have any secrets about your relationship with money?

46. If so, are you willing to share them now? If not, why not?

47. Do you have any self-forgiveness work to do relating to your history with money?
48. What would your spending look like if you were working for the well-being of everyone?

Let your responses rest for a day or so before going back to see how closely what you wrote expresses the gist of your own unique experiences with money. Don't be surprised if your first effort at writing your truths leads you to dig even deeper, into more profound levels of truth.

ALTERNATING NEW MUSCLES

Writing about money is tiring for anyone, no matter how physically muscular you are. Such self-examination requires a certain focus of mind, focus of will and focus of feeling. It uses "muscles" that get tired. The more you do it, of course, the more your muscles develop and the longer you can write without feeling worn out.

This is a good time to turn to the spiritual guidance part of Sabbath Economics. Take a break. Alternate between actively writing and receptively resting. Take a few days off, or a few weeks. Your money-love story has no deadline. Loving yourself contemplatively uses different muscles and lets the writing muscles rest.

Alternating between contemplation and action serves a number of purposes, besides allowing sore writing muscles to recuperate. It accomplishes some of the revising and polishing your money-love story will eventually require. Rest can also rekindle excitement in the Sabbath Economics project. When we're in it for the long haul, contemplative practices give the deeper parts of ourselves space and time to think differently about money and love.

Writing a money autobiography is hard work. It stirs up emotional muck, as well as meanings we have never noticed before, let alone named or claimed. Reflective writing works in the deeps, where a host of unconscious demons lurk in the shadows. When we stop awhile and step back to contemplate our story, these deeper parts get to rest and reflect without having to produce anything. We have time to mull things over.

PAIRED SHARING

Being seen and heard happens one person at a time.

In conversation with friends, notice the story *behind* their story

When we compare notes on what it means to be alive with love and money, we build bonds of trust and become friends on the journey.

Sprinkle conversations with pauses so you can breathe deeply.

Think of someone in whom you sense a story behind the superficial story.

What threads do you already see?

How might you pull one thread and uncover a deeper truth waiting to be heard?

BECOMING
BOTH / AND

Rather than seeing peace as a static 'end state,' conflict transformation views peace as a continuously evolving and developing quality of relationship.

John Paul Lederach

"YOU BOUNCED ANOTHER DAMN CHECK!" Her tone was accusatory. "This situation is SUCH a mess." She became more vehement. "Our finances are just too complicated." Pitch and volume went up another notch. "There are way too many things going wrong lately and I have no idea how to fix it."

He stopped in the kitchen doorway, braced against the familiar onslaught. He hated it when she complained about money, especially when she sounded like a whiny child. Her tone of voice made his head ache. It reminded him of his mother.

She sharply pulled air in through her nose and opened her mouth.

"Stop," he demanded. "Don't say another word." He raised one palm like a traffic cop. "Just STOP!"

"I hate it," she shrieked, "when you...

He folded his raised hand into a fist and shook it at her.

She lifted a skillet from the stove and aimed for his face.

Do you hear and see the escalating levels of conflict here?

Signs of uncertainty and complexity?

Points of saturation?

When we've had too much, some of us fight. Some take flight.

Others freeze. Some step away briefly to calm down, and then try to find a quick fix to make the complexity go away.

With this couple, neither is sure exactly what is going on. Both feel they have little or no control over what is happening. They probably see conflict as the enemy. They probably distrust complexity and think the solution to their money troubles lies in simplifying their joint account. They most likely have contradictory love-money expectations.

No wonder love-money troubles cause interminable headaches. No wonder many of us believe the remedy lies in avoiding conflict, or wading into it with fists and skillets. These two were friends before they became lovers, but now they're on the verge of turning each other into enemies.

As Abraham Lincoln observed paradoxically, "The only way to truly get rid of an enemy is to make him your friend." But how in the world do we make friends with complexity?

A contemplative approach to Sabbath Economics offers tools to help you and me develop greater capacities to cope with challenges like these.

A check bounces.

The bank charges a hefty fee.

The shared household account goes into the red.

Both partners go into tailspins of anger, blame and confusion.

How can we develop a *both/and* approach to money-love conflicts?

What will equip us to understand each other's upset without getting tangled in each other's fears and judgments?

START IN THE LIGHT

Begin by envisioning the hot-button issue as a window suffused with light. Once a window is in place, most of us hardly notice the glass, because we look through it to focus attention on whatever lies beyond the window. And we almost never notice the light flowing effortlessly through the glass.

Sabbath Economics reminds us to focus on windows and light rather than being drawn into someone's fiscal-anxiety spin-cycle.

Windows and Light are more than a metaphor. When we shift our attention to view the inevitable money-love complexity of partnership as a double-paned window suffused with light, we are gifted with two lenses through which we can look afresh at apparent contradictions.

One lens brings the *content* into focus — the bounced check — while the second lens helps us see the *context* — our partner's emotional reaction. Gazing in the Light, through this double-paned window, we become able to take seriously the fiscal ramifications of a bounced check — without getting tangled up in the shadows of shame and blame.

How can you and I develop capacities for peacemaking with partners, and *at the same time* avoid getting panic-stricken or overreacting?

Start by formulating *both/and questions* instead of settling for *either/or* options. Framing the issue in *both/and* does two things: it acknowledges the underlying energies that could lead to conflict, and at the same time, it aids in developing an integrative response. *Both/and questions* equip us to turn enemies into friends by holding paradoxes together.

NEJGHBORING

Never doubt that a small group of thoughtful,
committed citizens can change the world; indeed, it's
the only thing that ever has.

Margaret Mead

RASHEDA of BANGLADESH

BURNED SLUM IS A CLUSTER of tin and bamboo shacks in Kalyanpur, Bangladesh, where everyone uses the open gutters as toilets. Some men work in factories or construction sites. Others work as trash pickers, lorry drivers or rickshaw pullers. The women of Burned Slum work as domestic helpers and they all cook outdoors. Like most Bangladeshis, the families barely get by, earning less than a dollar a day.

Five years ago, the only source of water for Burned Slum's five hundred families came intermittently from a tap that was illegally connected to the city water facility. Women and children had to stand in line for two or three hours to collect a pitcher of water. Some tried to collect a bucket of water from the nearby houses, but this was dangerous because of the risk of being beaten by caretakers.

We had to rise very early in order to get water for the family, reports Rasheda Begum, a 25-year-old garment factory worker. *We often incurred the wrath of husbands and in-laws when we were delayed. There had to be a better way to get our water.*

Slum dwellers have no social power, but this did not stop Rasheda. She gathered the women together and asked them to work collaboratively toward securing a legal *"water point"* connection in the neighborhood. Mr. Mohammad Nurul Hudu Mian, manager of the water agency, insisted that water could only be provided to legal land-title holders or house owners. The slum women held no titles and owned no property, but they refused to give up. They sent a delegation to DSK, an organization formed to promote health, clean water and sanitation in collaboration with the United Nations Development Programme. Once the UN got involved in Bangladesh, things changed. "The law still doesn't permit it," Mr. Mian admitted, "but the rules are now relaxed a bit, due to social considerations."

Now Rasheda and her neighbors enjoy bathing with water from a well dug right behind their shack. For drinking and cooking, they obtain fresh water from the slum's new *water point* consisting of two hand pumps that draw from an underground reservoir.

"Persistence pays," says Rasheda, "when women collaborate. Our husbands are less frustrated because we are no longer delayed in obtaining water, so there is much less domestic violence."

RUTHANN, JAN and LAILA of CHICAGO

When she opens the refrigerator after work, Jan and her two children find three meals already assembled. Three friends agreed to each prepare a single, large meal to feed each other's families. One meal goes into the cook's refrigerator. The rest are packaged up and exchanged on Sunday evenings. "It's like eating at a restaurant, only you take whatever the chef has cooked," says Ruthann. "When we get our meals, everything is in the bag, including directions about how long it will take to cook or reheat."

Cooperative cooking arrangements take many forms. Each Sunday, I make a big batch of Sabbath Soup, concocted from organic vegetables picked fresh at the Farmer's Market, and share the overflow with neighbors who are ailing or grieving. Laila organizes ten families in her neighborhood to cook and swap meals once a month. Ruthann and Jan belong to a 'pick-up' group of cooperative cooks who prepare and eat meals separately in their suburban homes. Potlucks and shared-meal groups also thrive among residents of apartments, co-housing communities and college campuses across the country.

Cooking co-ops support healthy, green, economical food choices. Making one big meal for a crowd requires less money, less planning and less prep time than cooking five to seven meals for one's own family. Collaborative cooking minimizes the temptation to dine out, purchase expensive convenience foods or settle for fast foods. Ethnic traditions are often shared, inspiring participants to try out special recipes. And co-op cooking frees up the food budget to buy in bulk.

Some groups accommodate vegetarians, some cater to self-identified "*foodies*," and others cook local, organic and/or vegan. Each form of cooperative meal-sharing means that each cook spends less time shopping, preparing and cleaning up, and enjoys more time for talking, laughing and connecting over food with family and friends.

"Cooking co-ops are a perfect example of the ways that greening a whole category of purchasing can work," says Alisa Gravitz, Co-op America's executive director. "An organic, local apple may cost more than a conventionally grown apple, and Fair Trade Certified™ vanilla may cost a bit more than conventional vanilla. But if you cook cooperatively, then the savings on your food budget from buying in bulk makes it possible to green your remaining food purchases. By thinking about the category of food holistically, you can eat greener, healthier, and more varied meals—at the same cost as your old way of eating."

BETH of DETROIT

When she moved to inner city Detroit, Beth embraced everything about urban life except the guys who ran the tattoo parlor on her block. She was young and petite, so Beth felt intimidated every time she encountered the yelling, punching, and shoving that often took place on the sidewalk near the tattoo parlor.

Eventually Beth decided to face her fears by getting her own tattoo. She walked in and told the guys what kind of tattoo she wanted. "I want *Love Thy Neighbor* right here." She placed her palm on the counter and pointed at the skin just above her right wrist bone.

"Love thy neighbor!" The owner scowled in astonishment "I've never had no one ask for that before. Why you want that?"

Beth was ready. She expected the question, and quickly explained that she was having trouble loving her neighbors, because they acted so rude and rough on the street in front of her apartment. All the guys in the shop fell silent. Then one tattoo artist poked the owner with his elbow. "Manuel, dude, we're scaring our neighbors. We gotta stop fighting."

Beth winced at the pain, but was pleased with the design. She could only afford to pay for a black-ink tattoo, but the artist added red to a rosebud he threw in for free, and green to the leaves and stems he entwined around the words *Love Thy Neighbor*.

From then on, the men did not fight on the street, and Beth felt safer in her neighborhood. A few weeks later she ran into Manuel on the next block. He surprised her by giving her a big hug, and saying proudly to his friend "See, this here is my neighbor. She's the one I was telling you about."

PAIRED SHARING

Team up with a friend or colleague and tell each other about:

- A time I witnessed people collaborating for the greater good...
- Was it planned in advance, or impromptu?
- What did I notice as I watched and heard them work together?
- A time that I took part in a collective collaboration...
- How did I get involved?
- How did things start? How did they end?
- What effect did this experience have on my self-respect?
- How did I express appreciation to my collaborators?
- What forms of satisfaction do I feel now, as I remember what we accomplished together?
- What kinds of generosity do feel I called to offer, these days?
- With whom might I be more generous?
- What sort of relational wealth might I discover as fruit of a collaborative action?

PART FOUR

AQUIFERS

TAKING STOCK

It all depends on everything.

Haitian proverb

You've done the hard part. You've taken a clear-eyed look at your life through the dual lenses of love and money, gifts and limitations. You've crafted a financial plan and put parts of it into motion. Perhaps you've even purged your urge to splurge. Maybe you've tightened your spending budget and expanded your savings. Perhaps you've switched your accounts from a for-profit bank to a community-based credit union. Maybe you've chosen to sink cash into repairing your old car rather than saddling your 'self' with a new car loan.

Whatever you've done, you have already accomplished the hardest part. You have begun to shift from operating on unconscious habit patterns toward bringing greater awareness to the ways you link love with money. Re-visioning your life, you have begun to approach dollars and details as thoughtfully as you would approach a dearly beloved person. You can now bring a wider attention and deeper *intention* to your personal interactions, as well as to your financial ones.

You have begun crafting fiscal plans with care instead of carelessness, and it feels good. You now bring greater presence to money matters. You are on your way toward being as genuine with credit card purchases as you are in paired-sharing with a good friend. Each spending choice is becoming as alive for you as a hot date. You more often feel the love energy that flows through your paycheck and your bills, and you appreciate managing the outflow of money as much as you appreciate receiving the inflow.

In the process of noticing and naming how far you've come on this journey with Sabbath Economics, you can more fully inhabit your own unique money story. You have not yet achieved full financial independence, but you have dumped a lot of bad habits.

Where are you now?

In the course of taking stock, you notice something is still wrong. You've made progress toward your goals, but don't feel fully contented. Something is incomplete, but you can't quite put your finger on it. You pause to reflect on it, but the effort makes you sleepy. Before long, you notice you have drifted off into a fantasy or a memory.

Maybe you pick up your copy of *Sabbath Economics.* You flip through the book to see what you might have missed or ignored. You land on the question about retirement planning. That's it, but every time you decide to research IRAs, you tend to drift off… so maybe there's still some hidden baggage around retirement? A certain dullness of mind drifts over you like winter fog whenever you think about old age. You find that any distraction is better than trying to figure out how to save money for retirement. It's too depressing to think about being too old to get a paycheck. You'd rather eat Doritos and watch the tube than track down someone who can help you set up a retirement account.

INVESTING IN
JUSTICE

*After years of uneasily grappling with the question
'What's my fair share?' I feel relaxed and blessed by the
resources I have to offer. I don't feel I have 'given up'
anything. I enjoy, instead, a pleasure akin to having
given a special gift to a loved one, a feeling of being
enriched and strengthened by taking part in something
larger than myself.*

– Christopher Mogil

M OST AMERICANS DO SHARE THEIR money, to some degree.
People commonly give from one to three percent of their
income to support charitable or religious causes. Ten percent is
considered generous. Fifty percent is extraordinary. Christoper
Mogil gave more than that.

CHRISTOPHER'S STORY

A phone call from a stockbroker's secretary shocked the young
man. "Don't hesitate to ask us if you have any questions about
your portfolio," she said.

Christopher was confused. "What are you talking about?"
She said he had just inherited money from his grandmother,
money he had no idea was coming. It was more money than
he could imagine. He was living on a meager income with a

community of social change activists in Philadelphia, and the unexpected inheritance left him conflicted. His head whirled with questions.

> *Why should I be this wealthy when most people are not?*
> *How can I take care of this money and not lose it?*
> *Should I spend it on myself, or make life easier for my friends?*
> *Should I use it to promote a better world? How?*

Christopher needed help. He wanted to ask family members for guidance.

> *How did you spend your money last year?*
> *How much do you give away?*

But such questions felt too threatening to his kin, and to himself. They were not willing to discuss personal finances. That's when Christopher, too, joined *the polite silence*. Still conflicted and curious, he learned about a network of progressive, wealthy people who gathered annually to talk about equality, democracy and philanthropy. He attended conferences of the Haymarket People's Fund in Boston, and The Funding Exchange in New York, but found discussion limited to investing assets and donating small portions of income to worthy causes. Rich people kept all of their assets. No one mentioned giving away principal until one spring day in 1986, a woman asked, *Has anyone seriously considered giving away our wealth?*

"There was a stunned silence," wrote Christopher, "except for my pounding heart. I raised my hand and was excited to see a few others raise their hands. Four of us met to share our stories. We were buoyed by the discussions, but uneasy about giving away a chunk of our assets. How would other wealthy donors advise us? Would they tell grisly tales of naïve generosity, followed by regret and bitterness? We wanted to learn how others decided to give away their wealth, and how they felt about it afterwards. As young inheritors, we wanted to avoid repeating the mistakes of our elders. *But how do you find rich people who have given their assets to social change? They don't advertise themselves.*

Christopher and his colleagues became amateur detectives. They spoke to a reporter from the New York Times, and a researcher on philanthropy at Boston College. Both sources pointed them toward people who were giving away assets. Christopher enlisted Anne Slepian, a progressive young inheritor, and they started asking hard questions of people of diverse ages, races and religions. None told disaster stories. All were thought-provoking accounts of what motivated them and how they found deeper security and greater meaning by giving money to causes that advanced their core values. The more wealth they gave away, the richer they felt. Forty interviews became a handbook that mixes stories, themes and exercises to rethink society's mindless quest for wealth, power and privilege. *We Gave Away A Fortune: Stories of people who have devoted themselves and their wealth to peace, justice and a healthy environment* came out in 1992. Christopher and Anne's book helps us all reconsider the role of money in our lives, culture and economy. I cherish these stories and offer highly condensed versions of accounts given by two women I knew personally.

JOAN'S STORY

In 1984, Joan went on a pilgrimage to Haiti, guided by Ministry of Money. There she helped care for the poor. Powerfully moved by her experience, Joan reflected on the injustice of poverty and received a new sense of what made her life rich. Determined to act on her realizations, she 'invaded' the principal of her revocable trust and bought a building in a major east coast city. She had it converted into a care facility for homeless men who fell ill.

Joan's testimony: *I have seen the Spirit at work and I have seen men loved back to health by people with caring hands and hearts. I, in turn, have been loved back to health and freedom in ways I never experienced before — by these very men. Co-creating with God set me free.*

TRACY'S STORY

Tracy's mother was a Pillsbury. Her stepfather was a Gary, whose grandfather invented the dial telephone. Her parents traveled most of the year, and Nellie cared for Tracy from infancy in her family's thirty-room mansion. A chauffeur took her to school. By helicopter, her parents visited Tracy at boarding school; at graduation, they picked her up in a yellow Rolls Royce.

"When I was eleven, I asked my stepfather how much Nellie was paid for working sixty hours a week with almost no time off. I was shocked to learn that my beloved caregiver earned only seventy-five dollars a week, plus room and board. Without Nellie, I would not have become the caring, generous person I am. Something in me snapped when I learned the huge incongruity between what Nellie had and what my parents had."

When I met Tracy in the late Eighties, she was founding director of The Women's Foundation in San Francisco, where she ran programs to help women manage inherited wealth. I lived near Golden Gate Park, and Tracy liked to meet me at the Arboretum for long walks and talks. In one meadow abundant with wildflowers, small signs reminded us to "Stay On Path." She and I laughed and repeated those words each time we saw another sign. *Stay on Path.* That became the motto of our friendship.

I remember some of Tracy's money-love stories. At age six, she was ceremonially presented with her first quarter, and taught to manage an allowance. At twelve, her mother took her to the bank to open a checking account, and taught some basic bookkeeping. "I never heard my parents talk about money," she said, "never saw them pay a bill or display concern for the value of anything."

When she was fourteen, they told her she had a trust and would never have to work.

At twenty-one, Tracy took a class on money management and was scared to realize how much she didn't know. She was motivated to learn quickly because a patronizing trust officer addressed answers to Tracy's questions to her brother. "I was determined to learn how to get proper attention," she said. She asked her mother's attorney to explain the family trust, and learned she would be getting chunks of wealth at 25, 30, 35 and 40. It was more money than she would ever need. Clearly, she could afford to give some away.

At 25, Tracy decided to give away half. Although she said it wasn't *bad money,* she recognized that her wealth was made off the backs of hardworking people who received no profits from the companies that benefited from their labor. By giving principal, Tracy chose to give back much of that profit.

"I've been able to afford therapy to heal and grow," she told me, "and I've learned the value of caring, connectedness and intimacy from my non-profit work. These relationships sustain my mental health. I prefer group decision-making. In order to bridge our differences, we need to listen respectfully to each other's experiences. Social change only happens when we really hear each other's truths and digest them, not just react.

"My experience is as important as yours," she said, "but having more money does not give me more weight in the decisions we make together. I like being connected with people who put love and money into social change. It gives me the precious gift of greater awareness of myself, my community and my world."

Tracy played a key role in starting the National Network of Women's Funds. Her work across the nation has fulfilled a lot of dreams. Over the course of two decades, she came to understand that her time is more limited than her money, so now she budgets time as well. Every year in late January, she rents a house on the shore of Lake Tahoe and goes there alone on retreat. She looks back over the previous year and records where she put her time and energy. She looks carefully at each aspect of her work, and how she feels about it. She looks at each strategy she employed, and assesses how effective it was. "Mostly," she says, "I meditate, give thanks and pray for guidance and world peace."

QUESTIONS FOR REFLECTION AND DISCUSSION

- From *We Gave Away a Fortune* by Christopher Mogil and Anne Slepian:
- If someone gave you $100,000 to give away, what would you do with it?
- How do you decide how much to give?
- What do you like about the way you give?
- What would make it more fulfilling?
- Have you experienced your giving making a difference? How?
- If not, what motivates you to keep giving?
- What doubts and concerns do you have about your giving?
- How could you resolve them?

WHAT DO YOU REALLY WANT?

Mechthild of Magdeburg, a mystic in the Middle Ages, described what the soul desires and also what God desires in this prayer (found in a volume on Beguine Spirituality):

> *God, you are my lover,*
> *My longing,*
> *My flowing stream,*
> *My sun,*
> *And I am your reflection.*
>
> *This is how God answers the Soul:*
> *It is my nature that makes me love you often,*
> *For I am love itself.*
> *It is my longing that makes me love you intensely,*
> *For I yearn to be loved from the heart.*
> *It is my eternity that makes me love you long,*
> *For I have no end.*

SORTING OUT OUR DESIRES

What did I really want when I returned from my first immersion in the hard realities of life among the Haitian people? I had no idea.

What did God want from me, and for me? I had no clue.

Wrenched, awakened and deeply touched by relationships with Haitian religious leaders, peasants and *ti machan*, I needed a chance to reflect and breathe. I also needed people who could listen to my stories and help me make sense of the startling new insights and deep longings that came to light under that Caribbean sun. At age fifty, I had discovered a new world of systemic racism and monetary classism. But it was not a new world, of course. Racism and classism had always been there, but I was blind to them, and blind to my part in perpetuating them.

I returned home from Haiti with a disquieting new self-image as a white woman of privilege. I had never seen myself that way before. My self-understanding was not new, either. This self-image had been hiding in plain sight until Haiti's people opened my eyes, and my mind, my heart and soul to the heart-breaking fact of my own place in the system of inequality from which they had suffered for generations. That experience of disequilibrium thrust me into a new stage of my spiritual journey.

I needed to figure out what it all meant. And I really needed to find out what I truly wanted. I needed help to sort out so many conflicting desires. But first, I faced a dilemma.

When I was a young adult, Buddhist thought and meditation practice informed my soul. But Buddhist doctrine rejects desire. I had taken on the perspective of my Buddhist teachers, who held that all forms of wanting take us away from the present moment. I learned from them that human desires are dangerous because they propel us into cravings that can never be satisfied. According to the Buddha, desire is the cause of all suffering.

Christian mystics, on the other hand, teach that habitually suppressing our true wants keeps us in the dark. Unless we probe our hidden desires, we may never discover the true core of longing that leads us more deeply into union with God. Contemplative Christian teachers recommend that we intensify our desires to the point of transparency. This is necessary inner work, but it is not a do-it-yourself project.

SOUL WORK

The fruit of silence is prayer
The fruit of prayer is faith
The fruit of faith is love and
The fruit of love is silence.

Mother Teresa

THOUGHT OF MYSELF AS A woman of faith, but it still did not come naturally for me to take money into prayer. I prayed about health and relationships, but not finances. I did not know how to be honest with God because, deep down, I was still mad at my parents for not being honest with me. They spanked me for lying, but hid their own lies and secrets until long after I had made some financial whoppers of my own. I was given no financial autonomy as a daughter, or as a wife. Growing up without healthy models of economic and spiritual interdependence led me to invent a deadly pattern of *faux* independence. After the divorce, I *liked* controlling my own money and stubbornly refused to give up my purchasing power, even to God. I set my jaw and held onto the pretense of control for an embarrassingly long time, despite cycles of anxiety and heavy financial pressure. Each time I faced a tough fiscal decision, I would swing from one extreme to the other, either obsessively calculating and refiguring the costs and benefits, or impulsively spending or giving away too much.

Could I be what the prophet Isaiah meant by *a stiff-necked people?*

MEETING MY SEVEN DWARVES

Not until I entered into soul work with a trusted spiritual guide was I able to get more honest with myself. It began when she asked which fairy tale came to mind when I thought about my relationship with money.

Gloomy and Grumpy showed up immediately, chanting *Hi-Ho, Hi-Ho, it's off to work we go.* Graspy was next, revealing the hidden part of me that felt so unloved and so broke that she held on too tight to whatever did come along. Behind Graspy marched Denial and Dorky, shouldering shovels and doing their best to bury my financial problems in the unconscious. Sleepy's job was to snooze through all my troubles with both love and money and act like everything would be fine in the morning. And finally, Sneaky showed her face. She had been part of me since that shoplifting incident at age twelve, and she continued to stay on duty while I raised my family. It was Sneaky who taught me to hide the U-No candy bars inside a lima-bean box and keep it in the freezer so the kids wouldn't discover Mom's secret stash of sweets.

I could hardly believe it when my dear spiritual director asked how I might take the Seven Dwarves into prayer. Didn't she get it? I could barely acknowledge their existence, let alone take such secretive characters to God. As if the Omniscient One didn't already know me inside and out...

Gradually, given enough tricky questions and caring guidance, I stopped hiding in the dark with my seven dysfunctional dwarves. After a while, I could even let Sneaky and her sisters drink from the well of Love. Their financial, emotional and spiritual freedom drenched me, too, with Living Water. Given enough human and divine assistance, I could relinquish old fairy tales and illusions of control. I could accept my parents for doing their best, despite giving me insufficient training in money matters. Some of it was misguided — and some of it was just plain wrong. So what? It was time to quit blaming the folks, forgive them their debts, and move on.

Holy listening in the presence of a skilled spiritual director led to clarity about vocation as well as finances. I decided to invest time and money in learning the ministry of soul work, and have practiced it now for forty-some years. Now that my hair is turning gray, I actually enjoy bringing money to God. When I feel restless, I see it as an invitation to pause and seek direction. When I am prayerful, I get intuitive leadings about love and money, a gut sense of rightness or wrongness about particular financial choices. When I trust my inner sense, even when it doesn't fit the advice of experts, things usually work out for the best. When I get a clear sense of direction, I follow it. When that is lacking, I take it as a sign to wait in the Light until clarity emerges.

Soul work slows us down. It allows us time to pause and clean our glasses. Soul work invites us to rub our eyes and ask, *How can I use my time and talent and treasure and tenderness to do the greatest good?* Sometimes holy listening surprises us.

Mercy Center in Burlingame was just south of San Francisco, where I lived. I was delighted to receive an invitation from Sister Mary Ann Scofield, RSM, to join a handful of local religious leaders to talk about forming a national — perhaps even international — body of Spiritual Directors. She greeted us as *friends of God, and prophets,* quoting the Book of Wisdom 7:27.

In a small room on the ground floor of Mercy Center, sheltered by the branches of ancient oaks, thirty people of faith gathered to hear to Sr. Mary Ann's vision. She said she felt called by God to widen the circle of skilled listeners who felt called to accompany and guide others in matters of the soul. I remember her vision paralleled the purpose of the American Medical Association for doctors. SDI would have a similar mission: to support, train, supervise and provide ethical guidelines for those called to the vocation of spiritual direction.

A small, white-haired nun, she spoke in a soft voice, and we listened contemplatively. Some of those *friends of God* present asked clarifying questions, others distilled bits of wisdom out of the comments offered by those within the contemplative circle. We all served as midwives that day, a small group of listeners who assisted in bringing Spiritual Directors International to birth.

In 2002, Sister Mary Ann included a short history lesson in her symposium address. (The full text was first published in Presence Journal that year, and reprinted recently in the March, 2020 edition of Presence.)

"Thirty years before SDI came into being, spiritual direction was primarily the domain of ordained clergy; it was largely a Catholic phenomenon, and it occurred primarily within the sacrament of confession or some other private setting with a priest. Thirty years ago, it was quite bold to imagine spiritual direction being done by the non-ordained — and downright brazen to imagine spiritual direction being done by women! Yet that is precisely what God's spirit seemed to have in mind, and so it came to be: a worldwide reality that is now marvelously ecumenical and inclusive of people from all religious traditions. It happened first at the margins and gradually became accepted and then, in a sense, *popular.*"

Spiritual Directors International has grown exponentially over the past three decades.

Soul work has, indeed, gone mainstream and become popular. I have gained immeasurable gifts from studying the art of spiritual direction with masterful teachers. I have grown immeasurably in *bodymindheartsoul* by being *heard into speech* by masterful listeners. As a seasoned Spiritual Director, I feel privileged each time a troubled soul chooses to confide in me. Over the course of forty-plus years, I have been blessed to witness many unique inner journeys. As people entrust me with their struggles and insights, their pains and growth, their questions and confusions, I see them literally becoming *friends of God, and prophets.*

The journey of Sabbath Economics parallels the journey of soul work. Neither are do-it-yourself projects. When grace breaks in, we are given eyes to see injustices which we were formerly blind to. We all need help to stay true to a conversion process, whether it begins suddenly, as mine did in Haiti, or gradually, as it does for most. Transformation in matters of love and money usually requires some form of spiritual guidance and support. We find that we are called to do things differently as our values change… and as some of our most vital relationships either dissolve or deepen.

Sister Mary Ann Scofield summed it up beautifully:

In our wonder-full, perilous journey with God, we first become friends of God. Second, we are transformed such that we see things, people, events, indeed all of creation, from God's perspective. Third, we stay with this ongoing conversion, this prophetic stance, as it turns life upside down — or, more precisely, as all hell breaks loose!

QUESTIONS FOR REFLECTION AND DISCUSSION

- When was the last time you asked yourself what you really want?

- What came to mind?
- How long did you allow yourself to entertain that longing?
- Thirty seconds? Two minutes?
- What voice did you hear warning that whatever it was that you wanted, how could you have been so foolish as to think your desire could be satisfied?
- At what point did you judge yourself selfish or willful?
- Were you tempted to bury your barely perceptible longing for intimacy with God by settling for some form of consumer goods? Which kind?
- Who might you go to for help sorting out what you truly want?
- Who might listen respectfully to your concerns?
- Who might give your inchoate desires the space to become conscious and available to you, even enlarged and expanded?

QUIETING

Learn to be silent. Let your quiet mind
listen and absorb the silence.
Pythagoras

THE OLDER I GET, THE quieter I become. Drawn to stillness since I was a girl, I always lived in noisy households with dear ones. It has been a lifelong struggle to find enough quiet. Now widowed for three months, as much as I miss Sweet Pete's warm presence beside me in bed, I truly cherish the quiet. It is, finally, enough.

All religious traditions value silence. In the *Tao Te Ching*, the *Tao* is described as *the Great Way of stillness, for lack of a better word. The quiet flows, circles, flows and circles. And it has no name.*

Krishnamurti agrees. *This quietness, this silence is the highest form of intelligence, which is never personal. It is never yours or mine. Being anonymous, it is whole and immaculate.*

Lao Tzu describes silence: *The ten thousand things rise and fall while the Self watches their return. They grow and flourish and then return to the source. Returning to the source is Silence, which is the way of Nature.*

Rumi writes: *Sit quietly, and listen for a voice that will say, Be More Silent.*

QUESTIONS FOR REFLECTION AND DISCUSSION

- In what seasons of your life have you most been drawn to prayer and meditation?
- Under what circumstances do you forget to be quiet?
- What helps you return to stillness?

INTENTIONALITY

> *We enter the quiet with our scattered intentions and divided hearts. If we are not possessed of a unified intentionality toward God, we must at least be possessed of some particle of what Gerald May has called 'willingness,' to have our divided hearts given over to God, to have our scattered purposes unified in an intentionality toward God, to have our inner life repatterned and centered on God — as indeed it has always been at the deepest level.*
>
> Patricia Loring

INTENTIONALITY goes deeper than simple intention. Intentionality is the unseen current that directs a river to follow its course to the sea. It is persistent and consistent. For you and me, personal intentionality gives direction to whatever we do. Deeper still, intentionality is shaped by the force that draws us forward. It is the guiding current that determines what we yearn for. It is how we move toward our true purpose in life. At the deepest level, intentionality patterns us inwardly.

- Where do you sense scarcity in your life? Of what?

- What might fill those empty spaces?
- How might God be inviting you into stillness?

STILLING THE NOISE WITHIN: A SABBATH PRACTICE

Quiet has become a phantom memory. Some generations have no memory of it, because quiet has been driven out by noise pollution. Even in Small Town, USA clamor blares every hour of every day. Shouting has replaced reason. Screaming has replaced family conversation. The problem with being deluged by constant noise is that we become accustomed to listening only to sounds outside ourselves. Silence is missing in the human mix, for we are saturated with information, sated with noise and short on reflection.

Sister Joan Chittister

You and I *can* choose to be quiet.

This practice is adapted from *Simple Ways Toward the Sacred*, by Gunilla Norris.

- Choose a bowl from your cupboard, an empty one.
- Select a bowl you like, with a shape, color and texture that pleases you.
- Find a comfortable place to sit, with back supported and feet on the floor.
- Feel the rim with your fingers. Run your hand around the inside.
- This bowl embodies limits. It can only hold what it can hold.

- What are you holding these days? Anything beyond your limit?
- Wait. Listen inwardly.
- Notice what comes to you in the quiet.
- Place the empty bowl in your lap.
- Close your eyes and let the quiet settle upon you.
- Each time you are interrupted by a noisy thought, lift the bowl to your chest.
- Notice how solid it feels against your heart, how stubbornly truthful.
- What are you refusing to hold these days? Something that is yours to hold?
- Notice what comes to you in the quiet.
- Rest the empty bowl in your lap.
- Open your hands, palms up. Rest them on your thighs.
- Open your heart to the Beloved.
- Become a receptacle of grace, open and ready to receive.

SEASONS

The soul — with its insistence on finding the stillpoint from which it keeps rising — carries us through all the seasons of our lives.

Mark Nepo

- Writing in your journal, describe the season you are in now...
- How is this cycle impacting your *heartmindbodysoul?*
- *Go outside*, suggests Mark Nepo, *or sit near a window.*

- Breathe slowly and watch this season unfold around you.
- What do you notice?
- Close your eyes.
- Look inward and watch this soul-season unfold within you.
- Feel it brighten as it guides you closer to the still point.

HOLDING IN
THE LIGHT

*One of the noble bonds of love is how we lift each
other from the sorrows that press on us when we're
shut down by pain.*

Mark Nepo

"WILL YOU HOLD ME IN the Light?" I asked my friends. We were in Carol's home, eating the spinach-onion omelet she had cooked for us. During the meal, I told them about a heated confrontation I'd had with my daughter. I blurted when I should have paused, and the words I said to her in the heat of anger caused my beloved — and only — daughter to react by cutting off contact. She refused to answer my email messages, and when I finally phoned, I learned that she had blocked my number. I had been agonizing privately over this awful estrangement for a while, but this was the first time I confided the painful details to others.

"How can we help?" asked Janet.

"I could sure use a hug." My voice came out shaky.

"I will hold you in my arms, and in the Light," promised Carol. She quickly rose, opened her arms and murmured, "Come here."

I gratefully stepped into her embrace and leaned my head against her shoulder. Gail and Janet came around to our side of the table and enfolded us in their arms too. I could feel the throb of tender care as my shaky body absorbed their warmth and love.

Janet assured me, "We will hold you and your daughter in the Light for as long as it takes for you and Penelope to sort out this misunderstanding. What else do you need?"

"Please pray for the Beloved to guide me in making amends to my daughter, and to help soften Penelope's heart so she can hear my apology, receive my love and forgive me for trespassing against her."

That morning, my three dear friends continued to hold both of us. They held Penelope and me in their arms and in their hearts as roobios tea cooled in our mugs. Carol added a little rocking motion to our four-way hug, and a tuneless hum. We hummed *Amazing Grace* while holding and being held in the Light, rocking gently in a simple rhythm that soothed my soul.

To hold one another is the oldest form of heart-to- heart resuscitation, wrote Mark Nepo. Holding someone who is in pain, despair or sorrow invites the absent life-force to return. Holding and being held lets light back into a grievous situation. Letting in the Light may not be the final cure — or in fact, keep us from dying — but it is at the heart of all healing.

Michael is a dear friend with an innate gift for holding me in light and love. I consider him a friend because — unlike Carol, a Friend who belongs to the Religious Society of Friends — Michael belongs to no religious group and claims no particular spiritual tradition. He reads widely and explores huge concepts. He designs books, websites and social-media marketing strategies for authors like me. Michael expresses himself in words that often send me to the dictionary, but we rarely meet on the same sacred-language page.

He is, however, gifted with a keen intuition. It alerts him

when I most need to be held. Sometimes he physically shows up at my door and draws me into a wordless, healing hug. When I was stuck in the rehab hospital learning to walk again after a compound ankle fracture, he showed up with food, hugs and a listening ear. Over the years that my husband's health was failing with Parkinson's Disease, Michael accompanied me from a distance, faithfully inquiring how I was doing each time we were hit with a new caregiving challenge.

And on New Year's Eve, as I kept vigil with Pete during the last night of his life, Michael held me from afar. He kept in touch via text messages. "Trace infinity loops over his heart with your hand," he suggested sometime before midnight when I asked what could I do? This was exactly the right way to support Pete as he moved toward eternity, but I would not have thought of it without help. For many hours, I cupped my husband's dear head in my left hand, and lightly traced infinity loops across his chest with my right fingertips. When his breath went ragged, I reassured Pete that he was breathing exactly the right way to reunite with the cosmos. When I grew weary, the Beloved renewed my strength through deepened contemplative prayer. I was led to murmur *Light and Love, Light and Love* for hours as I traced continuous infinity loops over Pete's failing heart.

Holding others in the Light comes with infinite variation. You and I do not hold people in the same way, nor should we. Diversity in spiritual practice is as basic as diversity in human temperament, skin tone, eye color, and vocal range. Experience teaches me that participating in divine Love and Light is necessary, not only at the bedside of my dying husband, but in every situation I encounter throughout this wounded world of ours.

Our wounds often determine our preoccupations. If suffocated in childhood as I was, we long to be free. If neglected by our parents as both Pete and I were, we want to be touched. If wounded deeply enough, we tend to forget what is true about everything except our wound. Our traumas can carry so much weight that they press us into forgetfulness. Preoccupied with our own soreness, we forget our place in the Great Mystery. We may even forget there is a Mystery.

—————

Anchor Committees call us back to our ultimate anchor in God. Among members of the Religious Society of Friends, those called to varied forms of prophetic ministry can call together a support or anchor committee to help discern next steps and hold us accountable to a community in which all members participate in the prophetic process. I cherish the caring attention of the four Friends on my anchor committee who hold me in the Light as I prepare this manuscript for publication. They ground me in love and pose queries that call me back to my ultimate anchor in God. These Friends help me test leadings, brainstorm approaches to complex problems, and offer practical help along the way

For me, the path toward wholeness involves admitting when I cannot Do *it MYSELF!* I still find it very hard to ask most people for help, but I do trust friend Michael. For him, the path of holding means offering acts of service, so when it came time for me to venture behind bars and hold long overdue conversations with my friend Rosie on Death Row, he offered to drive me to the Central California Women's Facility in Chowchilla. Michael was not approved to visit and could not accompany me behind bars, so he waited four hours at the edge of the prison grounds in a trailer staffed by Friends Outside. Although we were separated by concrete walls, steel gates and electrified fences, I felt Michael's *holding presence* palpably while I was inside. His care and attention steadied me in Light and Love through two days

of grueling confessions from Rosie, who remains imprisoned in
guilt, hopelessness, depression and despair.

⎯⎯⎯⎯⎯⎯

A month after that, Friend Oliver asked me to hold *him* in Light
and Love while he led a two-day symposium at San Diego Zoo
Global's Institute for Conservation Research. Dr. Oliver Ryder
is Director of the White Rhino Genetic Rescue Program. He
had summoned geneticists, biologists, ethicists and journalists
from around the world — plus the animal-tenders from the zoo
next door — to consider the best next steps to protect the noble
Northern White Rhino from extinction.

My good friend Michael volunteered to arrange lodging
and drive me to Safari Park. Most significantly, he offered to
sit beside me during the two days of proceedings as notable
thinkers deliberated over the social, scientific, genetic, and ethical
issues of rescuing such a rare species from extinction. It was my
rare privilege, as a Quaker elder to *stay anchored in the presence
of God*. Michael's presence steadied me to hold a wide range of
impassioned speakers in Light and Love without getting tangled in
their individual perspectives. Together he and I supported Friend
Oliver, who chose to use clear, unbiased Quaker Process to guide
participants through a serious exploration of the risks and benefits.
All present raised questions and expressed emerging views and
values in a collaborative effort to help the Southern White Rhino
recover, with their cutting-edge human help.

The truth is, you and I are created of free will. We are free
to hold others in the Light, or decline. Free choice is embedded
in our very Essence. Wholeness is our birthright and our legacy,
but is never forced upon us. You and I must choose to hold and
be held. It may mean letting go of lesser desires. It may mean

surrendering old fears and bad habits to the Light as we choose a path of freedom. The path of wholeness always welcomes us. All we need to do is follow it.

Stay On Path.

(I can hear Tracy Gary's bright laughter accompanying that invitation.)

PAIRED SHARING

Arrange a time and place for conversation with someone who doesn't have an agenda for you, someone who does not expect you to speak or act in a certain way, someone who isn't afraid that your ideas might upset some personal apple cart.

Sit with someone that you trust to listen to you without getting emotionally reactive.

Describe a time when someone tenderly held you…

How did it affect you to be physically held?

Describe a time someone asked you to hold him or her…

What was this experience like for you emotionally? Spiritually?

Call to mind someone you know who is now struggling with something… How might you hold him or her in a time of anxiety, confusion, or sadness?

QUAKER WAYS OF HOLDING

Accompanying one another in the light takes many forms among Friends. Margery Post Abbott reminds us of some:

Prayer Partners, occasionally or on an ongoing basis.

Clearness Committees to aid individuals in discerning where God is calling them.

Peer Groups that meet regularly to encourage one another in steady spiritual practice.

Elders who pray for Friends, encourage individual gifts and convey the Quaker tradition through example and teaching.

Anchor/Support Committees that offer spiritual and practical care, and hold ministering Friends to account.

MYSTERY OF LIGHT

Light is that Creative Power that first dawned on chaos and that draws all things upward into nobler states of being. It is also warm, living and personal, forever pleading with us to give up our selfish desires and desiring us to follow its Divine Leading.
Howard Brinton, Quaker Educator

Friends originally called themselves *Children of the Light*, for the transforming power of light is central to Quakers. *Children of Light* refers to the Light of Christ described in the first chapter of John's Gospel. Quakers see the Light of Christ as available to all persons, whether they know Jesus or not. They understand the Light as being both guide and monitor.

Sabbath Economics practitioners can learn from stories of transformation in the Light that have happened to those who preceded us. It is challenging and hard to integrate love and money in the twenty-first century. Contemplative practices in the Mystery of Light are hard and breathtaking and astonishing for us, just as they were for our ancestors. We need their stories of transformation to help us remember where we came from, who we are, and how we are still joined in the heart of the Beloved.

Every story reminds us that we, too, are radiant but broken. Love and Light still ask us to gather the gifts that come out of hardship and to keep our hearts and minds open to grace. Integrity asks us to continually widen our circles of compassion to include those on the margins. No matter what challenges we face, the Light invites us to stay tender and resilient and resourceful, so that we will not be tempted to harden our hearts.

Seventeenth-century Quaker ancestors had good reason to be wary of the Light. In the early years of the Religious Society of Friends, few regarded the Light as the source of joy, peace of guidance that later generations have come to welcome. Today's perspective is optimistic, but early Friends, including founder George Fox, experienced their former lives as being *ripped up by the Light*. Founding Mother Margaret Fell captured the daunting nature of the light in this letter: "Now Friends, let the Eternal Light search you…For this will deal plainly with you; it will rip you up and lay you open, naked and bare before the Lord God from which you cannot hide yourselves. Therefore, give over the deceiving of your souls."

Samuel Caldwell listed fifteen characteristics of Light as identified by Quaker founders:

1. Divine — not equivalent to reason or conscience; not 'natural.'
2. Single — one and indivisible, not my Light vs. your Light.
3. Unifying — brings us into unity, draws Friends together.
4. Universal — works in the life of every person.
5. Eternal — existed before time and will exist forever.
6. Pure — perfectly good, unerring, and infallible.
7. Unchanging — our awareness of the Light changes, but the Light itself does not.
8. Personal — not an abstract force.
9. Inward — implies action, dynamic; the Light shines *within* each one of us.

10. Saving — brings us into right relationship with God, ourselves, and each other.
11. Guiding — will lead us into a more meaningful, richer life.
12. Resistible — we are free to ignore the guidance of the Light.
13. Persistent — our perception of the Light may dim, but we cannot completely extinguish it.
14. Empowering — will empower us to do what is required, even if we feel inadequate.
15. Ineffable — cannot be fully understood and described.

By the eighteenth century, it was less harrowing and dangerous to be a Quaker. In Philadelphia, William Penn captured the spirit of the times when he wrote, "For of Light came sight, and of sight came sense and sorrow, and of sense and sorrow came amendment of life."

In individualistic, twenty-first century America, those of us who seek to follow the path of Sabbath Economics may hear that contemplative prayer is private or narcissistic. It may look that way from the outside, with each one wrapped in personal silence. But testimonies across religious traditions give us a peek into secrets discovered by saints, mystics and spiritual guides across the ages.

I am here to remind us that contemplative practice on the path to Sabbath Economics is not just some private holiness trip. I am certain that intentionality with love and money shines through the stories in these pages. The energetic power of the Light has a profound impact on our broken and beautiful world, our broken and beautiful selves and our broken and beautiful neighbors.

I like the poetic way monk Thomas Merton describes the radiance in everybody:

If we could see it, we would see billions of points of light coming together in the blaze of a sun that would make all the darkness and cruelty of life vanish completely.

Merton makes it clear that access to this radiance is not at our command, however. We can enter it only through the gateway of contemplative stillness.

Buddhist scholar Mosu Kokushi confirms the path from an Eastern perspective:

Every sentient being possesses a spiritual light drawn from the Storehouse of the Great Light.

WHAT RINGS TRUE?

Money can be hard on our souls. It's hard on us to love money, hard to need it. Money taxes our understanding, challenges our integrity, and oppresses our spirits. Its impact on our lives is wide and its roots are deep. There's wisdom to be found in our experience, and in our Quaker testimonies, to help us engage ever more faithfully with this troubler of our souls.

Pamela Haines

I SAW MY FIRST LIST OF Quaker testimonials posted on a refrigerator in the kitchen of a home where a Quaker couple gave me shelter when I was homeless. It was a period of great vocational, economic and romantic turmoil for me. The man I loved as a soul-mate broke our engagement to pursue a younger woman. The ministry team that I had trusted conspired against me, shattering my trust in "men of God."

"Is your trust broken like a leg that will mend over time," asked my Conference Minister, "or broken like Humpty Dumpty?"

Totally shattered. Humpty Dumpty.

And now I had no home. No income. No lover. No job.

Where was solid ground?

Susan and Michael offered a room of my own so I could heal and regroup. As I stood in their kitchen, sipping tea and waiting for my soft-boiled eggs to cook, I saw a SIMPLICITY page held to the refrigerator with magnets. At the top were words written by Thomas R. Kelly in *A Testament of Devotion*, 1941: *Life is meant to be lived from a Center, a divine center... a life of unhurried peace and power. It is simple. It is serene. It takes no time, but it occupies all our time.*

The Simplicity Testimony went on:

"A life centered in God will be directed toward keeping communication with God open and unencumbered. Simplicity is best achieved through a right ordering of priorities, maintaining humility of spirit, avoiding self-indulgence, resisting the accumulation of unnecessary possessions, and avoiding over-busy lives."

My weary soul rejoiced. That morning, I read the queries while eating my eggs and toast, and returned to them each time I prepared a meal. Quaker wisdom was the nourishment I needed. The queries rang true.

- Do I center my life in an awareness of God's presence so that all things take their rightful place?
- Do I live simply, and promote the right sharing of the world's bounty?
- Do I keep my life uncluttered with things and activities, avoiding commitments beyond my strength and light?
- How do I maintain simplicity, moderation, and honesty in my speech, my manner of living, and my daily work?
- Do I recognize when I have enough?

Queries, I learned from the copy of *Faith and Practice* on a bookshelf in my room, are "a set of questions based on Friends practices and testimonies, which are considered by Meetings and individuals as a way of both guiding and examining individual and corporate lives and actions. Queries to be considered regularly are included in Faith and Practice; others may be formulated by a committee or Meeting that seeks to clarify for itself an issue it needs to address, or to invite other Friends to examine their beliefs and actions about a concern."

A *Testimony* is "(1) speech or action which derives from and demonstrates deeply held beliefs; (2) a commonly held, fundamental belief of Friends which has, over time, guided public speech and action, e.g., testimonies of equality, simplicity, community, integrity, and unity." (*Faith and Practice: Pacific Yearly Meeting of the Religious Society of Friends,* Pasadena CA, 2001

The following month, Susan posted the testimony of Integrity and Personal Conduct from Faith and Practice:

> *…let your yea be yea, and your nay, nay.*
> James 5:12, King James Version

"Integrity has always been a goal of Friends. It is essential to trust, and to all communication between people, and to all communication between people and God. Integrity grounds our beliefs, thoughts, and actions in our spiritual center, and makes us whole.

"Friends believe we are called to speak the truth. A single standard of truth requires us to conduct ourselves in ways that are honest, direct, and plain, and to make our choices, both large and small, in accord with the urgings of the Spirit. It follows that we object to taking any oath which presupposes a variable standard of truth. Be true to your word."

The queries on INTEGRITY:

- How do I strive to maintain the integrity of my inner and outer lives?
- Do I act on my principles even when this entails difficult consequences?

- Am I honest and truthful in all that I say and do, even when a compromise might be easier or more popular?
- Am I reflective about the ways I gain my wealth and income, and sensitive to their impacts on others?
- Is my life so filled with the Spirit that I am free from the misuse of alcohol and other drugs, and of excesses of any kind?
- Do we, in our Meeting, hold ourselves accountable to one another as do members of a healthy family?

Friends' Integrity Testimony rings true for Pamela Haines, a lifelong Quaker active in Philadelphia Yearly Meeting's Economic Justice Collaborative and Friends Economic Integrity Project. When she was growing up, her father taught classical economics and wrote a textbook entitled *Money and Banking*, whose royalties, by the way, funded college for the six Haines kids. A stickler for accuracy in household accounts, Dr. Haines taught his daughter to ask big questions.

"A conversation got me wondering, Did I have a right to a refrigerator? What if I came to the point where I felt I couldn't do without one? If I believed I was entitled to a refrigerator, would that put me on the wrong side of a struggle about equality and right sharing someday?

"Would I find myself protecting my refrigerator — and the rest of my possessions — from those who had none?"

Pamela's parents were newly convinced Quakers when she was young, proud of their values, but prone to judging people who spent money on luxury items. Over time, she heard her father question basic assumptions of the theory on which his textbook was built. He gradually become an outspoken critic of the classical economics on which he had based his working life. "I had struggles with my father," she said, "but witnessing this evolution in his thinking was a big gift. I learned that I, too, had a right to look around in this territory, even without formal training. I had a right to notice things that seemed inconsistent, a right to use the language, and a right to ask questions."

Questioning is part of the Quaker birthright. "I want everyone to feel they have this right," Pamela wrote. "I want everyone to be able to freely explore the territory of economics and come to feel at home there. Our world is in sore need of people of faith who are as outspoken about economics as they are about war and peace."

FOCUSED CARE

I also grew up with a father who was outspoken on economics, though he attended only one year of high school. His father was president of a bank that failed in the wake of the 1929 economic crash. My dad had to drop out of Benson High School early in his sophomore year and drive delivery trucks to support his parents and three younger siblings during the Depression.

Pamela's father was a professor who taught economics. Mine was a milkman. Hers wrote textbooks. Mine delivered dairy products to porches. Both managed money with great care. Focused care goes well beyond vocational labels and educational levels. Focused care transcends overalls and work boots, or white shirts with dress shoes.

Investing loving energy into savings plans, and investments in organizations that match our values is the foundation of focused caring. In discussing money matters with my dad, or hearing him expound on what was wrong with the economy (plutocrats and Republicans), I could feel love energy flowing through his words and raising his volume. I could see the heat of passion reddening his face as beads of sweat popped out across his forehead. No *ummms or ahhhs* cluttered Dad's exhortations on the stock market or the politicians who messed with it. The psychic heat of eros is a soul force. In my Dad, it moved through every word he spoke and every stock he bought or sold. He linked love with money and crafted our household budget with care, not carelessness.

Discussions with her father took a different form for Pamela, but I can readily imagine Dr. Haines also crafting financial plans with care rather than carelessness. I imagine he also invested classical economics with the soul force of love, condensing and cleansing his views and values over time.

My dad concentrated intensely on tiny columns of figures printed in the Wall Street Journal as he sussed out the meaning of each rise and fall in the value of stocks that interested him. He fiercely linked intention with attention where money was concerned. My image of Dad is that he caressed dollars and fiscal details the way he caressed my mother's sweet, soft skin. I could see the pulsations of energy in his temples as he hunched toward the TV screen, watching daily market reports and assessing risks and benefits until the Stock Exchange closed down for the day, and sometimes for a while after. That stuff rang true to him.

Stock fluctuations do not make my heart beat faster. In fact, I drift off immediately when faced with columns of figures. My eyes glaze over when I read quarterly investment reports and household asset class allocations. And the fact that I am afflicted with a *numerical dyslexia*, which causes a dullness of mind with regard to facts and figures is a definite sign that I am not suited to handle my own money. Luckily, I recognized this disability early enough to seek financial help. Grace guided my way to certified financial planners who invested the same degree of focused care into my retirement account that my dad — and also Pamela's — brought to household economics.

In 2017, Pamela Haines spoke on "Money, Integrity and Community" to Friends at the Intermountain Yearly Meeting. In 2018, she published *Money and Soul*. In Pendle Hill pamphlet #450, she asks, "So, what do we do with all this? How do we find our way as investors and debtors and workers and citizens — as Friends — through this tangle of knotty issues? How do you and I navigate the political economy in which we swim?"

The conscientious manner of Quaker living often puts Friends at odds with the dominant culture. Economic issues pervade Friends' testimonies. Pamela wrote:

"Quakers value integrity, yet our economic system has no place for conscience.

We value simplicity, yet our growth economy requires ever-increasing consumption.

We value equality, yet we see economic inequality increasing dramatically.

We value community, yet our society throws out those on the margins.

We value good stewardship, yet we are running through resources, soil, clean air and clean water, at an alarming rate.

We value peace, yet the violence and devastation cause by our economic system's exploitation of people and the planet is tragic."

What rings true? Pamela Haines suggests navigating our personal and political economies by posing this question every step of the way. She suggests testing each fiscal decision we make against the framework of Quaker testimonies. *What rings true?*

Pamela grew up in Philadelphia, near the Liberty Bell. She participated in peace vigils in front of that iconic bell, so it became more than a metaphor for her. The Liberty Bell strikes me as a symbolic way to gauge what we do both in private and in public. If the voice of our inner guide is stifled like a bell whose clapper has been disabled, broken, or wrapped in flannel. We are left unable to hear values like simplicity and integrity ringing in the clear fresh air. Fiscal decisions and actions do ring true, however, when you and I keep our liberty bells free of impediments. This way, when as we make choices with love and money, we can hear the Quaker values embedded in our actions.

PAIRED SHARING

Invite a trusted friend to join you for tea. Agree to converse as if you are both unmuffled bells, ringing true.

- How do we become more attentive to our internal state and condition when we sense something that carries the ring of truth?
- What do you notice now about the elements in a situation that rang true?
- Describe a time when you gave or received a gift that felt exactly right.
- Tell of an interaction with someone that felt so simple and so true, you'd love to relive it.
- What do you think made that exchange possible?
- What did you contribute to the moment?
- What did the other person bring?
- How might we bring our experience of integrity to the economic sphere?

- How do we speak to *that of God* in others when dealing with financial problems?
- What might be a good next step in aligning fiscal actions with simplicity?
    - Equality?
    - Integrity?
    - Community? o Stewardship?
    - Peace?

HOW THEN SHALL WE LIVE?

As READERS BORN IN THE United States, most of us have a stubborn tendency toward rugged individualism. We like to keep our God private, one-on-one, and we like to keep our money private, tucked safely into wallets and bank accounts. But when we glimpse *that of God* in others — and especially when we have direct first-hand experience with what Quakers call *the unity in the midst of commotion* — we come to realize how the Beloved is all about forming us into communities, rather than saving individual souls. Justice is about coming into right relationship with love and money for all people, not just us personally and maybe our buddies. Conversion to the path of Sabbath Economics always thrusts us into community relationships, for love and money are intimately interconnected.

Remember the *seed of God* implanted within. As you follow your light and do whatever is yours to do, your seed will crack open and blossom, in its own sweet time, and in increments you can bear.

No matter what we face with love and money, the Beloved reminds us to *harden not your heart*. Instead, we are invited, to stay open and resilient and tender through each conflict and resolution, each heartbreak and healing, each gift and loss. The Beloved persistently invites us to tend our souls as faithfully as we tend our gardens, our household chores and our finances. It means tending and mending our regrets as faithfully as we tend and mend our budgets and forgive our debtors.

None of this comes easy. Authentic grace never comes cheap.

To know God means to know what has to be done, said Jewish philosopher Emmanuel Levinas. And if knowing what has to be done involves Sabbath Economics, it means one's life will get turned upside down. Following this path is bound to set us apart from the way most people — including many of our nearest and dearest — see, think and feel. It made Saint Francis a laughing stock in his hometown. It landed George Fox and countless early Friends in prison. It pushed Dorothy Day to take actions of economic justice that most people found incomprehensible. It cost Gandhi and Martin Luther King, Jr. their lives.

"The best name for God is SURPRISE!" said Benedictine Brother David Stendle-Rast. Why? Because God is always doing something new, according to Isaiah 43:19. Being fortified for divine surprise requires us to become contemplative activists, for without contemplative grounding, we are likely to get stuck in anger at injustice, or pride in ourselves for our generosity. Contemplation links us to *that which is eternal* in everyone, including outcasts, strangers and all who are marginalized. Contemplative practice softens our hearts toward the lost and the lonely.

To be worth our salt, we must be rooted and grounded in faith communities that support us, help us discern the right next steps, and keep us accountable. Contemplative listening in the context of beloved community strengthens us to stick with the deeply spiritual work of structural economic change — for the long haul. So, notice and name the next step that appears before you in the light and *Stay On Path.*

QUESTIONS FOR FINAL REFLECTION AND CONVERSATION

Here are the last queries in a book salted with them.

With journal and pen, or in dialogue with someone, notice and name the seeds you water deep within:

- Seeds of Mind, thoughts and calculations and computations
- Seeds of Heart, emotions and memories and yearnings and hopes
- Seeds of Body, sensations and gut instincts and moments of direct knowing
- Seeds of Soul, of not-knowing and trust and openness to what is

HOW THEN SHALL WE LIVE?

The closing query, posed by Quaker ancestors, is regularly asked among Friends today.

How then shall we live?

I invite you to rest with me in the words of Ephesians 3:16–21, a passage I view as the original charter of contemplative activism:

I pray that, according to the riches of glory, God may grant that you be strengthened in your inner being with power through the Spirit, and that Christ may dwell in your hearts through faith, as you are being rooted and grounded in love.

I pray that you may have the power to comprehend, with all the saints, what is the breadth and length and height and depth, and to know the love of Christ that surpasses knowledge, so that you may be filled with all the fullness of God.

Now to the one who by the power at work within us is able to accomplish abundantly far more than all we can ask or imagine, to God be glory in the church and in Christ Jesus to all generations, forever and ever. Amen.

POSTLUDE

Empty as a beach, awaiting its gift from the sea.
                                    Anne Morrow Lindberg

Y*ou. You!*
The word carried a musical tone. The voice felt beckoning, not demanding. God's call to write this book came in a musical voice both serene and intellectually stimulating. It came three weeks after Pete's Memorial Meeting, on the third day of a medically supervised eight-day fast that I had undertaken to grieve, cleanse *bodymindheartsoul,* and listen more deeply for guidance from the Beloved. I took two queries into the fast:

> *Who am I to become now, as a widow?*
> *What am I to do with what remains of my life?*

Being nourished by nothing but water left me physically depleted. Trusting in God and sinking into extended periods of silence left me porous to *Something More.* I began to see that the covenant of love was saturating my consciousness the way seawater permeates a living sponge. Sponges do not create the water they hold. An ocean of love passes through the sponge the way contemplative prayer passes through the human heart and mind and pen and keyboard. For me, this creative process began with Sabbath practices that had already softened some of my hard edges. Contemplation prepares our *mindheartbodysoul* to soak up meaning from living waters that flow through it. The more fully we enter into this mysterious flow of love, the more we absorb the many mysteries that come our way. Sorrow and hunger had somehow mysteriously opened my ears to the *audible imagination,* a lovely term coined by poet Robert Frost.

What I heard was an invitation to revisit Sabbath Economics and write this spiritual guide. God's call came more like a musical score than a text. Divine harmonics proceeded to shape and compose the words; I followed a divine score that I could feel evolving, even as I wrote. That is, the words you are reading on these pages came from somewhere beyond myself. So, while I cannot claim full credit for the authoring of this book, I can tell you that I was faithful to a process of nurturing a seed tended by the man I married in old age.

TRANSFORMATIVE LOVE

The day will come when, after harnessing space, winds, the tide and gravitation, we shall harness for God the energies of love. And on that day, for the second time in the history of the world, man will have discovered fire.

Pierre Teilhard de Chardin

My beloved Pete was dying, and we both knew it. His body was failing, his language was disappearing and his memory was clouded. To remind him of his true nature, and to anchor him here on earth a little longer, I read aloud passages from Pierre Teilhard de Chardin. *The Divine Milieu* had guided his soul since the early Sixties. Pete discovered the Jesuit theologian in the library of an American military base on the remote island of Guam, where he taught high school history. Isolated from kin and consumer life in the United States, and bored by the booze-based social life on base, Pete took solace in the complete works of Teilhard. He credited that faith-based writer for teaching him how to live and love, how to cut through cultural illusions and face divine reality. The *energies of love* pulse at the very heartbeat of our relational wealth.

HOLDING IN THE LIGHT

For all our skills and training, you and I are left — finally — with our simple capacity for *holding*. My grandmother taught me to hold all creation in love, and she did it with few words. I watched her practice Sabbath at breakfast each morning as she listened to hymns and scriptures on the radio, while we sat at her kitchen table spreading homemade apricot-pineapple jam on toast. A devout woman who knew God loved her, she held me in love, and I felt secure in it. My grandmother practiced the most elemental form of covenant. *I am here for you. I see you and hear you. I love you.* Soul companions and spiritual directors do the same.

Holding is the heart of covenant. Sometimes all we can do is hold each other in light and love as we go through times of emotional pain, financial pain and relational uncertainty.

Sabbath Economics is a challenging practice, but holding and being held sustains us.

We wrestle with our history.

We name our hurts with love and money.

We identify what matters most.

We do our best to stay close to what we find most life-giving.

We learn to be better listeners to ourselves and to our God. *

We learn to listen more deeply to our neighbors.

We take the risk of revealing money-love secrets to friends.

We find ways to tease out deeper stories beneath the first

versions that others tell us. We develop a new, hard-earned vocabulary to describe truths long-hidden from view. We refresh familiar spiritual practices, and learn new ones to sustain us through the inevitable challenges and confrontations of growth with love and money issues.

We tend and mend our relationships with enemies, neighbors and dear ones.

We let everything integrate within us, some of it at the conscious level, but much more that is hidden beneath awareness.

Beneath all the dilemmas we face in negotiating complex emotional relationships, we discover that everyone is connected.

Behind all the conflicts we face in making healthier money choices, we discover how firmly all financial decisions can be rooted and grounded in love.

The more we remember to savor our essential *belovedness*, the fresher forms of resourcefulness and resilience spring forth from us.

No matter what story we find ourselves in at the moment, we listen and love.

We ask ourselves and each other, "So, what is the next step?"

A COVENANT OF LOVE AND PROMISE

Fiscal management relies on a certain kind of mentation, an intellectual orientation. It carries a certain rush that goes hand in hand with the rise and fall of the stock market. But the core of Sabbath Economics requires a different orientation, one that is the antithesis of society's cognitively-driven movements. Through the work of this spiritual guide, I want to move each reader not only into a different kind of thinking, but also into a slower mode of perception. You may have felt some of that varied pacing as you read through this book. Some of my stories mimic the racing pulse of their chapter's inherent narrative tension, while some of the spiritual practices may simply carry the beat of the heart at rest. You will find that your gears will alternate naturally in the transformative inner work of Sabbath Economics, as well as in the both/and movement between contemplation and action. That is because such rhythms will be intimately interwoven with the musical scores in each of your own love-money songs.

My invitation to you is to learn to shape and refine how you earn, spend, save and give of the resources entrusted to you. If you find the rhythmic patterns of your lifestyle choices are discordant, please ask yourself honestly: *Should they continue to be? Is that what you really want? Is that what your "higher power" wants?*

If the discordance seems to obviously match what is happening in your usual fiscal inflows and "outgoes," then I gently suggest you look to see if there is a similar discordance in the close relationship, or rhythmic beats if you will, of your consumption and contribution, your contemplations and your actions. No doubt, each of us can work more consciously to identify and follow our own unique tonal melodies where love and money is concerned.

For those willing to let go of certainty by yielding stubborn willpower to the guidance of Sacred Mystery, the covenant of love can guide us in surprising ways. For those ready to face emptiness — both scary emptiness and sacred emptiness — the covenant will embrace us. For those willing to take the battering that all mystics suffer *(if they don't quit)* — we remain stubbornly committed to the lifelong journey of relational wealth.

So, a covenant of love and promise is many things:
It is a useful guide to practices with love and money.
It is a tool of spiritual maturity.

It is a heartfelt agreement between our soul and
the Beloved.
It is an understanding shaped by each one of us,
even as we are being shaped and reshaped by the
Great Invitation of Jesus.

Covenants of love and promise are likely to disturb
the social status quo.
They upend our interior worlds.
Stuff rises into consciousness, stuff we have
forgotten, perhaps for decades.
They raise more questions than answers.

Forgiveness percolates upward.
Love dissolves old hurts layered into the deep
strata.
We stop collecting and start releasing.
We begin to change.

The tune of your Sabbath Economics Covenant will sound
different from mine because the lyrics and tempos of our gifts
and deficits are different. And your ideas, values, and practices
may have different syncopations than those of your loved ones.
Tomorrow's covenant composition will be different than today's,
and that is because God will be humming an ever-improving
tune in our ears, integrating something ever-more ancient to sing
within us. Daily time with the Beloved enlarges the spiritual
circumference of our fiscal choices. Circles of trust nourish us
more than whatever is on sale at the mall or available on eBay.
Living in cahoots with Holy Presence changes our fiscal and
relational priorities. The Way, the Truth and the Life brighten our
voices into a more harmonic consonance with our choral textures.

By the third version of our Sabbath Economics covenant, we respond more antiphonally to spirit than we did at the beginning, and more urgently, as every note follows more gracefully the one that preceded it, connecting us, yea as consumers and spenders, with that *Something Beyond*.

———— ～～～ ————

THE PEARL OF GREAT PRICE

The *pearl of great price* is another of Love's mysteries. In Matthew 13:45–46, Jesus' metaphor of the pearl is linked to the kingdom of heaven, but I claim literary latitude here to view it as a personal parable in the context of Sabbath Economics.

Consider the pearl, a treasure to behold. Consider the source, a humble bivalve mollusk that dwells on the floor of the sea and does its work in darkness. Pearls don't set out to be valuable. They begin as simple grains of sand. Oysters don't set out to produce pearls because they want to create something lovely. Oysters just want to stay comfortable, but when sand gets into their shells, they get irritated. They react to discomfort by secreting something that keeps coating each grain of sand until it becomes something less bothersome. So, it can be said that "oysterly persistence" is what brings those beautiful pearls into being.

The open secret of money-love transformation is that it works like oyster-pearl formation. The desire to acquire begins very early in North American children. Economic irritants build as we grow up. These irritants include unconscious habits and financial confusions that keep us captive to the seductions of consumer culture. Unchecked desires for money, stuff, and power can tyrannize us without our even noticing it, *let alone naming it.* Happy in our shells, soothing the irritants of life with small comforts, we can go on spending automatically, unconsciously piling up debt and accumulating yet more stuff, blithely unaware of the mounting relational and spiritual costs.

Like the gradual transformation from sand to pearl, human economic change is a byproduct of irritation and struggle. If pearl-making can be a song hummed by oysters, then we humans can let Sacred Presence inhabit us and flow through us like a musical score. May your own private *relational wealth chorale* resonate with illuminative transparency, lifting the hairs on your arms as mine did when I first heard Haitian *ti machan* singing those luminous canticles in praise to God. May your Sabbath Economics covenant intermingle love and money as naturally as water when living streams flow into oceans of light.

> *Then you will know the truth, and the truth will set you free… so if Love sets you free, you will be free indeed.*
> Gospel of John 8:32,26 NIV

RESOURCES
FOR FURTHER
EXPLORATION

Abbott, Margery Post, *Walk Humbly, Serve Boldly: Modern Quakers as Everyday Prophets*, Inner Light Books, San Francisco, 2018.

Acocelk, Joan, New Yorker Magazine, November 3, 2003.

Altman, Donald, *Meal by Meal: 365 Daily Meditations for Finding Balance Through Mindful Eating*, Inner Ocean Publishers, Makawao, Maui, HI, 2004.

Ambler, Rex, *Light to Live By: An Exploration in Quaker Spirituality*, Quaker Books, London, 2002.

Annan, Kent, Beyond Borders Newsletter, Norristown, PA, Fall 2004.

Ayres, Ian, "You Bet Your Life" in Los Angeles Times Opinion section, January 27, 2008.

Bacevich, Andrew J., *The Limits of Power: The End of American Exceptionalism,* Metropolitan Books, Henry Holt and Company, NY, 2008.

Bischoff, Michael, *The Healing Power of Stories,* Pendle Hill Pamphlet 454, Wallingford, PA, 2018.

Bowie, Fiona (Ed). *Beguine Spirituality*, Crossroads Press, NY, 1990.

Brinton, Howard H., *Friends for 300 Years*, Pendle Hill Publications, Wallingford PA, 1994.

Brown, Patricia D., *Paths to Prayer: Finding Your Own Way to the Presence of God,* Jossey-Bass, San Francisco, CA, 2003.

Brueggemann, Walter, *The Prophetic Imagination*, St. Mary's Press, Winona, MN, 1987.

Brueggemann, Walter, *Praying the Psalms*, St. Mary's Press, Winona, MN, 1984.

Brussat, Frederic and Mary Ann, *Spiritual Literacy: Reading the Sacred in Everyday Life*, Scribner, NY, 1996.

Brussat, Frederic and Mary Ann, *Spiritual RX: Prescriptions for Living a Meaningful Life*, Hyperion, NY, 2000.

Burstyn, Ellen quoted in *On Turning 50: Celebrating Mid-Life Discoveries*, by Cathleen Rountree, HarperCollins, San Francisco, CA, 1993.

Byasse, Jason, "Shopocalypse Now" in Christian Century Magazine, December 11, 2007.

Cameron, Julia, *The Right to Write: An Invitation and Initiation into the Writing Life*, Tarcher/Putnam, NY, 1998.

Chittister, Joan, *The Psalms: Meditations for Every Day of the Year*, Crossroad Press, New York, 1996.

Chopra, Deepak, "Metamorphosis" in Resurgence Magazine, Devon, England, No. 241, March 2007.

Christian Century Magazine, October 2, 2007, (Beth's tattoo story).

Colwell, Matthew, *Sabbath Economics: Household Practices*, Church of Savior, Washington, DC, 2007.

Conroy, Maureen, *The Discerning Heart: Discovering a Personal God*, Loyola Press, Chicago, 1993.

Cornell, Ann Weiser, *The Power of Focusing: A Practical Guide to Emotional Self-Healing*, New Harbinger Publications, Oakland, CA, 1996.

Cornell, Ann Weiser, *The Radical Acceptance of Everything*, Calluna Press, Berkeley, CA, 2005.

Dodson, Shirley, *Quakerism 101: A Basic Course for Adults*, Philadelphia Yearly Meeting, Philadelphia PA, 1992.

Dominguez, Joe and Robin, Vicki, *Your Money or Your Life: Transforming Your Relationship with Money and Achieving Financial Independence*, Penguin Books, NY, 1992.

Dominguez, Joe and Robin, Vicky, Financial Integrity: Transforming Your Relationship With Money, free handbook from http://financialintegrity.org.

Dossey, Larry, *Prayer is Good Medicine*, Harper, SanFrancisco, 1996.

Dyckman, Katherine Marie, SNJM and Carroll, Patrick L., SJ, *Inviting the Mystic, Supporting the Prophet*, Paulist Press, NY, 1981.

Edwards, Tilden, *Living in the Presence: Disciplines for the Spiritual Heart*, Harper and Row, NY, 1987.

Edwards, Tilden, *Sabbath Time: Understanding and Practice for Contemporary Christians*, Seabury Press, Minneapolis, MN, 1982.

Edwards, Tilden, *Valuing and Nurturing a Mind-in-Heart Way*, Shalem Institute for Spiritual Formation, Washington DC, 2010.

Empereur, James L., *Spiritual Direction with the Gay Person*, Continuum Publishing, New York, 1999.

Elizabeth, Esther. The poet invites contact at Estherwelizabeth@gmail.com

Faith and Practice: A Guide to the Quaker Discipline, Pacific Yearly Meeting of the Religious Society of Friends, 2001.

Fardlemann, Charlotte Lyman, *Nudged by the Spirit: Stories of People Responding to the Still, Small Voice of God*, Pendle Hill Press, Wallingford, PA, 2001.

Favor, Judith, *Haiti Through the Eyes of Faith: An Invitation to Invest in the Future*, PRISM Journal: America's Alternative Evangelical Voice, May/June 2001.

Favor, Judith, "Spiritual Practices Selected from Elizabeth Fry's Journals," Friends Bulletin, March 2007.

Favor, Judith Wright, *The Edgefielders: Poor Farm Tales of a Great-Grandmother,* CreateSpace, North Charleston, SC, 2013

Favor, Judith Wright, *Silent Voices,* Pilgrimage Press, Claremont CA. 2014

Fischer, Kathleen, *Women at the Well: Feminist Perspectives on Spiritual Direction,* Paulist Press, NY, 1988.

Gary, Tracy and Kohner, Melissa, *Inspired Philanthropy: Creating a Giving Plan,* Chardon Press, Berkeley, CA, 1998.

Gratton, Carolyn, *The Art of Spiritual Guidance,* Crossroads, New York, 1997.

Haines, Pamela, *Money and Soul,* Pendle Hill Pamphlet 450, Wallingford PA, 2018.

Holy Bible, New Revised Standard Version, Thomas Nelson, Inc., Nashville, TN, 1989.

Howell, Nancy, *A Feminist Cosmology: Ecology, Solidarity and Metaphysics,* Humanity Books, Amherst, MA, 2000.

Hueretz, Christopher L., *The Sacred Enneagram; Finding Your Unique Path to Spiritual Growth,* Zondervan, Grand Rapids, MI, 2017.

Jerusalem Bible, Reader's Edition, Doubleday, Garden City, NY, 1966.

Jones, Ellis, *The Better World Shopping Guide,* New Society Publishers, Gabriola Island, BC, Canada, 2006.

Jung, C.G., (Letters I and II, G.Adler, Princeton, 1975) quoted in Sabrin, Meredith, *The Earth Has a Soul: The Nature Writings of C.G. Jung,* North Atlantic Books, Berkeley, CA 2005.

Keiser, R.Melvin and Moore, Rosemary, *Knowing the Mystery of Life Within: Selected Writings of Isaac Penington in Their Historical and Theological Context,* Quaker Books, London, 2005.

Kennedy, Robert F., Speech at the University of Kansas, March 18, 1968, JFK Presidential Library.

Kidd, Sue Monk, *When the Heart Waits*, San Francisco: HarperSanFrancisco, 1992.

King, Ursula, *Women and Spirituality: Voices of Protest and Promise*, Penn State University Press, University Park, PA, 1993.

Kisley, Lorraine, *The Prayer of Fire: Experiencing The Lord's Prayer*, Paraclete Press, Brewster, MA, 2004.

Kokushi, Muso, quoted in Keiji Nishitani, *Religion and Nothingness*, University of California Press, Berkeley CA, 1982.

Kornfield, Jack, *A Path with Heart: A Guide Through the Perils and Promises of Spiritual Life*, Bantam Books, NY, 1993.

Lamott, Anne, *Plan B: Further Thoughts on Faith*, Riverhead Books, NY, 2005.

Lewis, Thomas, Amini, Fari and Lannon, Richard, *A General Theory of Love*, Vintage Books/ Random House, NY, 2000.

Martin, Marcelle, *Holding One Another in the Light*, Pendle Hill Pamphlet 382, Wallingford, PA, 2006.

May, Gerald, *From Cruelty to Compassion: The Crucible of Personal Transformation*, The Fetzer Institute Essay Series, No. 2, Spring, 2003.

May, Gerald, *Will and Spirit: A Contemplative Psychology*, Harper and Row, San Francisco, CA, 1982.

Merrill, Nan, *Psalms for Praying: An Invitation to Wholeness*, Continuum Press, NY, 2000.

Merton, Thomas, *Thoughts in Solitude*, Noonday Press/ Farrar, Straus and Giroux, NY, 1952.

Miller, Robert, Editor, *The Complete Gospels, Scholars Version*, Polebridge Press, Sonoma, CA 1991.

Mitchell, Stephen, *A Book of Psalms Selected and Adapted from the Hebrew*, HarperCollins, NY, 1993.

Mogil, Christopher and Slepian, Ann with Peter Woodrow, *We Gave Away a Fortune*, New Society Publishers, Philadelphia

PA, published in cooperation with the Funding Exchange, 1992.

Muller, Wayne, *Sabbath: Restoring the Sacred Rhythm of Rest*, Bantam Books, New York, 1999.

Myers, Ched, "The Gift Must Always Move: An Interview" in Inward/Outward: A Journal of the Servant Leadership School of the Church of the Savior, Washington, DC, Winter 2002.

Myers, Ched, Bartimeus Cooperative Ministries Newsletter, PO Box 328, Oak View, CA, August 2008.

Myers, Ched, The *Biblical Vision of Sabbath Economics*, Church of the Savior, Washington, DC, 2001.

Myers, Ched, *Who Will Roll Away the Stone? Discipleship Queries for First World Christians*, Orbis Books, Maryknoll, New York, 1997.

Neafsy, Jim, "Praying for Others: A Contemplative Approach," Presence: An International Journal of Spiritual Direction, September 2018.

New International New Testament and Psalms, Counselor's Version, Zondervan, Grand Rapids, MI, 1968.

Novey, Joelle, National Green Pages, Coop-America, Jan-Feb, 2008.

Ochs, Carol and Olitzky, Kerry M., *Jewish Spiritual Guidance: Finding Our Way to God*, Jossey-Bass, San Francisco, 1997.

Pagels, Elaine, *Beyond Belief: The Secret Gospel of Thomas*, Random House, New York, 2003.

Palmer, Parker J., *A Hidden Wholeness: The Journey Toward an Undivided Life*, Jossey-Bass, San Francisco, CA 2004.

Palmer, Parker J., *Let Your Life Speak: Listening for the Voice of Vocation*, Jossey-Bass, San Francisco, CA, 2000.

Patterson, Pat, *Doing Theology at Pilgrim Place*, Volume 3, Wasteland Press, Shelbyville, KY, 2008.

Progoff, Ira, *At a Journal Workshop: Writing to Access the Power of the Unconscious and Evoke Creative Ability*, Tarcher, Los Angeles, 1975.

Progoff, Ira, *The Practice of Process Meditation: The Intensive Journal Way to Spiritual Experience*, Dialogue House Library, NY, 1980.

Provance, Emily, *Spiritual Gifts, the Beloved Community, and Covenant*, Pendle Hill Pamphlet 461, Wallingford, PA, 2020.

Reeves, Nancy, *Spirituality for Extroverts (And Tips for Those Who Love Them)*, Abingdon Press, Nashville, 2008.

Rogers, Frank Jr., *Practicing Compassion*, Fresh Air Books, Nashville TN, 2015.

Ruether, Rosemary Radford, *Sexism and God-Talk: Toward a Feminist Theology*, Beacon Press, Boston, 1993.

Ruffing, Janet K., *Spiritual Direction: Beyond the Beginnings*, Paulist Press, NY, 2000.

Sarton, May, *At Seventy*, W.W. Norton, New York, 1987.

Schaper, Donna, *Sabbath Sense: A Spiritual Antidote for the Overworked*, Innisfree Press, Philadelphia, PA, 1997.

Shea, John, *Stories of God*, Thomas More Press, Chicago, 1978.

Solnit, Rebecca, "Now Showing: Democracy" in Orion Magazine, March/ April 2005.

Spretnak, Charlene, *The Politics of Women's Spirituality*, Anchor/ Doubleday, NY, 1982.

Stairs, Jean, *Listening for the Soul: Pastoral Care and Spiritual Direction*, Augsburg Fortress, Minneapolis, 1998.

Steere, Douglas, *Together in Solitude*, Crossroad Press, New York, 1982.

Suchoki, Marjorie, *God, Christ, Church: A Practical Guide to Process Theology*, Crossroads Press, New York, 1995.

Swennerfelt, Ruah and Cox, Louis, "An Eleventh Commandment?" in Friends Journal, August, 2007

Teilhard de Chardin, Pierre, *The Divine Milieu*, Collins, London, 1957.

Thompson, Marjorie, *Soul Feast: An Invitation to the Christian Spiritual Life*, Westminster/John Knox Press, 1995.

Thoreau, Henry David, *Walden*, New American Library, New York, 1960.

Thurman, Howard, *The Centering Moment*, Friends United Press, Richmond, IN, 1969.

Twist, Lynne, *The Soul of Money: Transforming Your Relationship with Money and Life*, W.W. Norton and Company, New York, 2003.

Underhill, Evelyn, *An Anthology of the Love of God*, Mowbrays, London, 1953.

Vennard, Jane, *Praying with Body and Soul: A Way to Intimacy with God*, Augsburg Fortress, Minneapolis, 1998.

Wagner, Nick, *Spiritual Direction in Context*, Morehouse Publishing, New York, 2006.

Wahab, Mollika, "Bangladesh Slums Demand Access to Clean Water" in Choices: The Human Development Magazine of the United Nations Development Programme, March, 2003.

What Would Jesus Buy? Documentary film directed by Rob Van Alkemade and produced by Morgan Spurlock, 2006.

Williams, Rosemary, *A Woman's Book of Money and Spiritual Vision*, Innisfree Press, Philadelphia, PA, 2001.

Wink, Walter, *Transforming Bible Study*, Abingdon Press, Nashville, 1983.

Zaru, Jean, *Occupied with Nonviolence: A Palestinian Woman Speaks Out*, Fortress Press, Minneapolis, MN, 2008.

www.ingramcontent.com/pod-product-compliance
Lightning Source LLC
Chambersburg PA
CBHW051640090526
44820CB00033B/2173